"Randy Clark, whose ministry has changed my life, and Mary Healy, one of my favorite Bible scholars, offer this work on spiritual gifts to both Catholics and Protestants so that the whole body of Christ might be equipped to continue the supernatural ministry of Jesus. Be ready to be inspired."

Dr. Tom Litteer, assistant dean,
Global Awakening Theological Seminary;
faculty mentor, United Theological Seminary

"This is an exceedingly important book. Randy Clark and Mary Healy show that the gifts of the Spirit have always been available to followers of Jesus, and we can experience them powerfully today. If you're going to read one book on gifts of the Spirit, I recommend this one."

David F. Watson, Ph.D., vice president for academic affairs
and academic dean, United Theological Seminary

"*The Spiritual Gifts Handbook* is written in a way that educates and inspires brilliantly. It is unique in that the two authors, Dr. Randy Clark and Dr. Mary Healy, represent very diverse segments of the Body of Christ—Protestants and Catholics. The beauty of their diversity is that they add strength to the other. Often, doctrines, teachings and personal convictions become compromised for the sake of unity, which isn't always bad. Yet in this case, it's the opposite. They fortify the other by adding to what's already being taught and understood, without sacrificing the essentials. This handbook is a great gift to the Church and will be used to train and equip the people of God for many years to come."

Bill Johnson, author, *God Is Good*, *When Heaven Invades Earth* and *The Power That Changes the World*

"This book will revive your expectation for God to work through you. You will also witness the power of the Holy Spirit to bring Catholics and Protestants together to speak with one voice. Healy and Clark are an example of unity in the Body of Christ, proclaiming Jesus as Lord in the power of the Spirit. I believe this book will bring many together with a common vision for the vital role of spiritual gifts in evangelization. My deepest gratitude to both authors for breaking down barriers to unity so that the world may believe that the Father has sent the Son to save us."

Neal Lozano, founder and director, Heart of the Father Ministries; author, *Unbound: A Practical Guide to Deliverance from Evil Spirits*

THE
SPIRITUAL
GIFTS
HANDBOOK

Other Books by Randy Clark

Anointed to Heal (with co-author Bill Johnson)
Authority to Heal (book and curriculum)
Baptized in the Spirit
The Biblical Guidebook to Deliverance
Changed in a Moment
Entertaining Angels
The Essential Guide to Healing (book and curriculum, with Bill Johnson)
The Essential Guide to the Power of the Holy Spirit
Eyewitness to Miracles: Watching the Gospel Come Alive
Finding Victory When Healing Doesn't Happen (with Craig Miller)
The Healing Breakthrough
Healing Energy: Whose Energy Is It? (with Susan Thompson)
The Healing River and Its Contributing Streams
Lighting Fires
Power, Holiness and Evangelism (compiler and contributor)
Power to Heal (book and curriculum)
Supernatural Missions (compiler and contributor)
There Is More!

Other Books by Mary Healy (authored and co-authored)

Baptism in the Holy Spirit (Doctrinal Commission of
International Catholic Charismatic Renewal Services)
Deliverance Ministry (Doctrinal Commission of International
Catholic Charismatic Renewal Services)
The Gospel of Mark (Catholic Commentary on Sacred Scripture)
Healing: Bringing the Gift of God's Mercy to the World
Hebrews (Catholic Commentary on Sacred Scripture)
Men and Women Are from Eden
Scripture, Mercy and Homosexuality
When Women Pray

THE SPIRITUAL GIFTS HANDBOOK

Using Your Gifts to Build the Kingdom

RANDY CLARK AND MARY HEALY

Chosen

a division of Baker Publishing Group
Minneapolis, Minnesota

Published by Chosen Books
11400 Hampshire Avenue South
Bloomington, Minnesota 55438
www.chosenbooks.com

Chosen Books is a division of
Baker Publishing Group, Grand Rapids, Michigan

Printed in the United States of America

ISBN 978-0-8007-9863-5

Library of Congress Control Number: 2017961450

Cover design by Darren Welch Design, LLC

18 19 20 21 22 23 24   7 6 5 4 3 2 1

We would like to dedicate this book to the men and women who have preached and preach the Gospel, with healings and miraculous signs following. In doing so, they have greatly advanced the Kingdom of God and have won for the Lamb who was slain the rewards of His suffering.

Contents

Acknowledgments

I want to acknowledge the tremendous help of my editor, Trish Konieczny. I love working with you. You make my work easier and my books better. I also want to acknowledge Jane Campbell, the editorial director of Chosen, for believing in me and encouraging me to write. The whole team at Chosen has been so helpful in this entire process.

I am so thankful that God brought my co-author, Dr. Mary Healy, into my life. You have enriched my understanding of what God has done through the Catholic Church, and what He is continuing to do. I thank God that for you, the subject of this book is not merely an academic interest; you are also being used of God to flow in the gifts of the Spirit, including healing.

I also want to express thanks to John Rolf, the media director of Global Awakening, for finding the videos documenting many of my stories and creating the URL for the playlist (www.globalawakening.com/spiritualgiftshandbook).

Finally, I want to acknowledge a very patient wife, DeAnne. Without your understanding, I would not have found the time to write. You sacrificed so much of "our" time to allow this book to be written.

Randy Clark

I would like to thank all those who have helped enkindle in me expectant faith for the Lord to work healings and miracles beyond all we can ask or imagine, including Damian Stayne, Patti Mansfield, Peter Herbeck, Dave Nodar, Father Mathias Thelen, Patrick Reis and especially Randy Clark. The two weeks I spent with Randy and his team in Brazil were truly life changing. I am also grateful for the excellent editorial team at Chosen Books, who are unfailingly gracious and helpful. And I thank the Lord for the extraordinary outpouring of His Spirit in our time, which is forging bonds of unity among Christians and revealing to the world His everlasting mercy.

Mary Healy

Introduction

Jesus was a man of joy—the most joyful person who ever lived. His heart's desire is that those who believe in Him would fully share His joy (see John 15:11; 17:13). But surprisingly, there is only one place where the gospels directly mention that *Jesus rejoiced*. There must have been a very particular reason for His joy at that moment.

The context of the passage shows the reason. At the beginning of chapter 10 of Luke, Jesus sent out seventy of His disciples, a wider group than the twelve apostles whom He had sent out earlier. Like the apostles, the seventy were given the privilege of sharing in Jesus' own mission. They were to go from town to town announcing the Good News, just as He had. He instructed them, "Whenever you enter a town and they receive you . . . Heal the sick in it and say to them, 'The kingdom of God has come near to you'" (Luke 10:8–9).

A short time later, the seventy disciples returned bursting with excitement: "Lord, even the demons are subject to us in your name!" (verse 17). Evidently, their labors had been fruitful. As Jesus had mandated, they had proclaimed the

Good News of the Kingdom not only in words, but in works of power that demonstrated the truth of the words. They had seen bodies healed and demonic bondages broken—works that could only be attributed to the supernatural power of God breaking into the world. What is more, not only had they witnessed these mighty deeds, they had *participated* in them. They had been the instruments of God's healing for the hurting and the oppressed.

It was hearing their "mission reports" that caused Jesus to be filled with joy: "In that same hour he rejoiced in the Holy Spirit and said, 'I thank you, Father, Lord of heaven and earth, that you have hidden these things from the wise and understanding and revealed them to little children'" (verse 21). In His human heart, the Son of God was thrilled to see His disciples receiving God's gifts like children and using these gifts to bring God's love to others. If you are a parent, you know there is no delight quite like seeing your kids' eyes light up with excitement as they tear off the wrapping paper and discover the presents that you carefully chose for them, and then watching as they start to ride the bike, or play with the doll, or build the Lego set. It is this kind of joy that Jesus must have experienced when He "rejoiced in the Holy Spirit."

Jesus then exclaimed, "Blessed are the eyes that see what you see! For I tell you that many prophets and kings desired to see what you see, and did not see it, and to hear what you hear, and did not hear it" (verses 23–24). The disciples' hearts were probably burning as they heard those words. For so many centuries God's people had been waiting, hoping and longing for the coming of the Messiah and the visible presence of God's Kingdom. What others had longed for, the disciples now *saw* with their own eyes. How privileged they were!

Does reading those words make you wish you could experience, even just a little, the amazing things experienced by the disciples who followed Jesus during His earthly life? The healings, miracles, demons being cast out, sinners being converted, relationships being restored, the Kingdom of God breaking in on earth?

The truth is that Jesus spoke these words not just for His disciples in first-century Galilee. They are His words to *us*, His disciples today. What Jesus did through His disciples then, He is still doing and desires to do through us. Just as in the earthly life of Jesus, so in the life of the Church in every age, the spread of the Gospel is meant to be accompanied by signs, wonders, miracles and gifts of the Holy Spirit that demonstrate the presence of the Kingdom.

The use of the spiritual gifts does not involve any special knowledge or techniques, just prayer and faith in the power of the risen Lord Jesus. Here are two examples of the gifts in action, both involving healing—one that took place at a healing service, and the other through an impromptu prayer. (Note that throughout most of this book, we collaborate as one voice, but in the sections marked **Randy** and **Mary**, we provide you with our individual insights and experiences.)

Randy: A woman in her thirties had had knee surgery after an accident. A metal bar and twelve screws had been inserted in her leg, and as a result she was unable to bend her knee or walk without crutches. The doctor had told her she could either amputate her leg or take morphine for the rest of her life. Because she could not stand, she had to change professions and now did manicures so she could sit at work. After all this, her husband left her with two kids. Many times, she would sit in bed with severe pain and could not go into the kitchen to feed herself.

When this woman came to a meeting, I showed a video of people who had had metal in their bodies after injuries—in their shoulders, knees, legs, arms and backs—and who had been healed. I told the crowd that I believed some people would be healed just watching the testimonies on the video. During the video, this young woman felt heat come into the injured leg. Then I asked for those who were at least 80 percent better, either with pain reduction or a restoration of movement, to wave both hands over their heads. She did not wave her hands, but there were many others who did receive a healing, either during the video or when I prayed right afterward.

At the end of the service, she came up to the front for more prayer. This time it was with the laying on of hands. When I began to pray for her, her leg began to shake visibly. She felt a force bending her knee, pushing her forward and down and causing her to kneel.

She told me, "I'm not doing this; something is moving me!"

Then she knelt for the first time since her surgery. As she was being prayed for over the next twenty minutes, she kept improving and continued to feel heat and energy in her leg. She began to try to move her knee. At first, it was only a very small degree of movement, but gradually more and more movement came into it. She then began to stand on the leg that she had not been able to put weight on. Then she began to walk without crutches. She was so filled with joy and utter amazement that she and my translator were both in tears of joy. That night, she walked home without crutches. She is healed.[1]

Mary: A young woman named Kate Hyne woke up one day with her body suddenly covered with painful red scales from her scalp to her toes. She immediately went to a doctor, who determined that it was a form of psoriasis resulting from a severe anaphylactic reaction to some unknown allergen. Later, an allergist confirmed that if she came in contact with the allergen again, her throat could close in about five minutes, which would render her unconscious and put her in danger of instant death.

Kate was devastated and scared. At her parish, she had been attending Alpha, a series of sessions exploring the basics of Christian faith. On the day of her allergist appointment, she went to Alpha in the evening and tried to hide her condition with long clothing and heavy makeup. But when everyone started to go home afterward, she broke down and cried. Her parish priest and some friends saw her, gathered around and began to pray over her in the parish hall. They were not people known for a gift of healing, just a group of people spontaneously praying for a friend in need. Kate recounts,

> All of a sudden everything started to get very hot, and for the first time in months I wasn't in pain. That was the last thing I remember, because I fell into the Spirit. While I was in the Spirit, I saw my arms outstretched in front of me. There was fire on my arms, yet the fire did not hurt. Instead, it was brushing the scales off my arms, and the scales were falling off!
>
> After I went home with my mom and sister, I went to change into pajamas, and when I saw my arms I screamed. They were completely clear! Not even a scar! My mom and sister ran to me, and I just held out my arms and cried, and

then they started screaming, too! We all cried tears of pure joy and dropped to our knees, thanking God on the floor.

My sister Esther said, "When you fell into the Spirit, I caught you by your knees. Your legs became so hot I almost let go, but then there was this pulse shooting up your legs."

We looked at each other with the same question, and in a blink, I took off my pants to see what else had happened. We all started happily screaming again! The area above my knees, where Esther had felt the heat, was completely clear. The scales on the rest of my legs had been reduced, and there were stripes up my legs that were completely clear.

We all started crying and praying, thanking God for healing me. In our excitement, we took pictures of my arms on a cell phone and sent them to those who had prayed for me.

I went to my dermatologist soon afterward, and she looked at me and repeatedly asked, "What has changed? What medicine are you on?"

When I told her what had happened, she stared at me in shock. All she could determine from her examination was that the scales had existed, but were now gone. My body began responding to medicine, we found what caused the allergy (fish and shellfish), and my life regained a sense of safety and normalcy. Thanks be to God!

We have written this book in the conviction that manifestations of God's grace and power like these are not meant to be rare in the life of the Church. They are part of the normal Christian life. From the Day of Pentecost onward, Christ has been pouring out His Holy Spirit to equip all believers with supernatural gifts for their mission of spreading the Gospel and building up the Church. These gifts are not just for specially qualified people or extraordinarily holy people. They are for every member of the Body of Christ, every "little ole me." They are available to all who are willing to let the Lord use them however He chooses, to be the instruments of His love in a needy world.

Why, then, don't we see such gifts in action more often? A major reason is that so few Christians know what the spiritual gifts are, how they operate, or how to activate them and walk in them. Some people are afraid of being radically dependent on the Holy Spirit and find it easier to rely on their own knowledge, skill or experience. Others don't think they are worthy of having the Lord use them in a powerful way. And many church leaders don't know how to cultivate and pastor the use of the gifts among the people they lead.

The purpose of this book is to demonstrate the remarkable evangelistic and church-building power of the spiritual gifts and explain how to activate them, both for yourself and for your church family.

This book is unique in that it is an ecumenical approach to the gifts, responding to the deep desire for unity that is stirring in many Christians today. We have written this book as a Protestant (Randy Clark) and a Catholic (Mary Healy) together, to show that it is possible for Catholics and Protestants to speak with a united voice about the spiritual gifts. Although our church traditions are very different, they actually share much in common regarding the work of the Holy Spirit.[2] There is also much we can learn from one another. Catholics have a two-thousand-year tradition of teaching and practicing the spiritual gifts, even though the gifts have at times been neglected. Charismatic Protestants have a zeal for evangelism and a high level of faith for supernatural manifestations of the gifts. As Pope Francis has noted,

How many important things unite us! If we really believe in the abundantly free working of the Holy Spirit, we [Christians] can learn so much from one another! It is not just about being better informed about others, but rather about reaping what the Spirit has sown in them, which is also meant to be a gift for us.[3]

The divisions among Christians are a tragic counter-witness to the Gospel, but in our time the Lord is breaking down these walls. What unites us is infinitely greater than what divides us, since what unites us is nothing less than God the Father, Son and Holy Spirit. "There is one body and one Spirit—just as you were called to the one hope that belongs to your call—one Lord, one faith, one baptism, one God and Father of all, who is over all and through all and in all" (Ephesians 4:4–6). Part of God's purpose in pouring out His Spirit in our time is to restore unity among Christians. The deepest work of the Holy Spirit is to unite the members of the Body of Christ in an unbreakable bond of love, founded on the love of God Himself.

Bearing united witness to Christ in the power of the Holy Spirit is all the more necessary in our time, in a society that has pushed God to the margins and is suffering the consequences. We are surrounded by the walking wounded—those who have been hurt by living in a fallen world, and especially by the fallout from a secularized culture, including broken relationships, broken families, neglect, abuse, crime and prejudice. Many people have a gaping void deep inside, a great ache of the heart that shows itself in all kinds of harmful ways. It is the wound of spiritual orphanhood—a sense of aloneness and lack of identity that come from not knowing the heavenly Father, who knows us perfectly and loves us unconditionally. The gifts of the Spirit are a balm to heal that wound. They convince even the most broken and hardened hearts that God is real, present and active in our lives. They are part of God's answer to the spiritual darkness of our times. Today more than ever, it is essential that in seeking to walk in the Spirit and His gifts, we walk in unity with one another.

Insofar as possible, we have sought to explain the spiritual gifts in a way that will be acceptable to both Protestants and Catholics. We recognize and respect the fact that we have theological differences, some of them significant. We also have differences in vocabulary. For instance, many Catholics use the term *charisms*, but the term *spiritual gifts* is more familiar to Protestants (and to some Catholics). Catholics speak of *evangelization*, whereas Protestants usually say *evangelism*. Catholics refer to *Saint Paul*, whereas most Protestants just say *Paul*. Catholics talk about being *made alive*, whereas some Protestants speak of being *quickened*. Catholics celebrate *the Eucharist*, whereas Protestants celebrate *the Lord's Supper*. We invite readers to extend grace to those of different Christian communions and not let unfamiliar vocabulary be a stumbling block. We are convinced that the Lord desires to pour out His supernatural gifts even more abundantly on both Catholics and Protestants, so that the King and His Kingdom may be revealed on earth.

I

What Are Spiritual Gifts?

It is the Holy Spirit who . . . bestows and directs [gifts] like jewels to the Church, the bride of Christ. It is in fact he who raises up prophets in the Church, instructs teachers, guides tongues, works wonders and healings, accomplishes miracles, grants the discernment of spirits, assigns governance, inspires counsels, distributes and harmonizes every other charismatic gift. In this way he completes and perfects the Lord's Church everywhere and in all things.[1]

In these exuberant words of Novatian, a third-century Christian writer, we see a vision of the Church as alive with the constant working of the Holy Spirit through gifts distributed among the members. These words summarize well what Scripture teaches about the immense value of the spiritual gifts.

The New Testament refers to the gifts of the Spirit in many passages, especially in the letters of Paul.[2] Paul coins a term for them: *charism* (*charisma* in Greek), meaning a gift freely bestowed.[3] It is based on the word for "grace" (*charis*). Grace is the foundation of Christian life: God's favor freely bestowed on us in Christ, saving us from sin and death and giving us a share in His own divine life. A charism is what might be called a "gracelet," a droplet of the vast ocean of God's grace. It is a tangible expression of God's grace in a person's life in the form of a capacity to act in a way that surpasses human power.

Scripture uses a rich vocabulary to describe the charisms. In 1 Corinthians 12:1–7 Paul uses no less than five terms. He calls them "spiritual gifts" (*pneumatika*, literally "spirituals") because they are given by the Holy Spirit (*pneuma*). They are "charisms" because they are given freely. They are "different kinds of service" because their purpose is to serve others. They are "different kinds of working" because every time we use a gift, the Holy Spirit Himself is working through us. And they are "manifestations of the Spirit" because they make the presence of the Holy Spirit evident to others.[4] The letter to the Hebrews uses yet another term: They are "distributions of the Holy Spirit" (Hebrews 2:4, literal translation) because the Spirit distributes them in different measure to different members of the Church.

Paul's strong emphasis on the close relationship between the gifts and the Holy Spirit shows that these gifts are not natural human abilities, but supernatural abilities the Holy Spirit gives to enable believers to be instruments of God's love and power to others. A natural gift, such as athletic ability or musical talent, is an innate aptitude that you can develop and use at will. But a charism is dependent on the operation of the Holy Spirit, and therefore it has an efficacy that surpasses merely human talent. It either enables what is humanly impossible (such as prophecy, healings or miracles), or it elevates a natural aptitude (such as teaching or administration) to a supernatural level of efficacy. We can grow in the use of these gifts, but they always remain dependent on the Holy Spirit. If you have a gift of healing, for example, you cannot pull that gift out of your pocket and heal someone whenever you feel like it. Rather, you are a musical instrument on which the Holy Spirit plays according to His purpose and His timing. The more yielded you are to Him, the more freely He will play.

Paul was convinced of the power of the gifts to open people's hearts to the Gospel. He was one of the most effective evangelists in history, yet he insisted that it was not primarily his preaching that won over so many people to Christ, but rather the supernatural deeds that God worked through him. He wrote, "I will not venture to speak of anything except what Christ has accomplished through me to bring the Gentiles to obedience—by word and deed, by the power of signs and wonders, by the power of the Spirit of God" (Romans 15:18–19). He reminded the Corinthians that it was such manifestations of the Spirit that convinced them to believe: "My speech and my message were not in plausible words of wisdom, but in demonstration of the Spirit and of power, so that your faith might not rest in the wisdom of men but in the power of God" (1 Corinthians 2:4–5). The Holy Spirit's action through the gifts provides visible confirmation of the truth of the Gospel.

Who Gets the Gifts?

Yet Paul in no way regarded such gifts as confined to apostles like himself. Rather, they are part of the ordinary life of the

Church. The charisms are gifts not only in the sense that God gives them to people, but that *their very purpose is to be used for others.* They are by definition gifts to be given away, to be used "for the common good" (1 Corinthians 12:7). They are a means by which God's grace circulates among the members of the Church and overflows beyond its boundaries. For that very reason, no one has all the gifts it is possible to have—because then we would not need each other. The charisms teach us to receive and give away God's grace, so that the Body of Christ functions as a living organism, each part contributing in a unique way to the whole.

> If the whole body were an eye, where would be the sense of hearing? If the whole body were an ear, where would be the sense of smell? But as it is, God arranged the members in the body, each one of them, as he chose. If all were a single member, where would the body be? As it is, there are many parts, yet one body.
> The eye cannot say to the hand, "I have no need of you," nor again the head to the feet, "I have no need of you."
>
> 1 Corinthians 12:17–21

The human idea of unity is uniformity—everyone thinking, dressing and acting alike. But God's idea of unity is a marvelous unity in diversity, each person contributing to the flourishing of the whole by using his or her unique God-given gifts.

Paul makes it very clear that charisms are given not only to some, but to all Christians: "To *each* is given the manifestation of the Spirit" (1 Corinthians 12:7, emphasis added). Every believer has an irreplaceable role to play in the growth of the Church; everyone is given charisms that perfectly correspond to that role. There is no unemployment in the Kingdom of God! Or at least there would not be, if everyone knew how to recognize and use his or her gifts. Scripture therefore emphasizes that exercising our gifts is not optional; it is a sacred responsibility. "As each has received a gift, use it to serve one another, as good stewards of God's varied grace" (1 Peter 4:10). Many Christians do not exercise charisms because they have no idea how to use them and grow in them; they may not even know what they are. This is a great loss to the Body of Christ.

Biblical Gift Lists

The letters of Paul include several lists of charisms. Some of these lists highlight the more extraordinary gifts, and some the ones that seem more ordinary. But all the gifts are powerfully effective for the building up of the Church. The longest list is in 1 Corinthians 12:8–10, which mentions the word of wisdom, the word of knowledge, faith, healings, miracles, prophecy, discernment of spirits, tongues and interpretation of tongues. Paul uses the term *spiritual gifts* for these, probably because these are especially dependent on inspiration by the Holy Spirit; they might be called "gifts of inspiration." For that reason, they manifest in an especially powerful way the reality and presence of God in the world. These 1 Corinthians gifts are the special focus of this book.[5]

In Romans 12:6–8, Paul speaks of prophecy (in common with 1 Corinthians 12), then adds gifts of serving, teaching, encouraging, contributing to the needs of others, leadership and showing mercy. These gifts are less flashy but equally necessary to the flourishing of the Church.

Paul gives a slightly different kind of list in Ephesians 4:8–11. He uses a different word for gift (*doma*), and then he lists apostles, prophets, evangelists, pastors and teachers.[6] These are not so much gifts of the Holy Spirit, but are individuals who are anointed by the Holy Spirit for a particular office in the Church. But these offices, too, are gifts in that they are given by the Holy Spirit to build up the Body of Christ.

In 1 Peter we are told that "as each has received a gift [*charisma*]" we should "use it to serve one another, as good stewards of God's varied grace [*charis*]" (1 Peter 4:10). Peter then follows this statement with the examples of two general categories: speaking gifts and serving gifts.

> If anyone speaks, they should do so as one who speaks the very words of God. If anyone serves, they should do so with the strength God provides, so that in all things God may be praised through Jesus Christ. To him be the glory and the power for ever and ever. Amen.
>
> 1 Peter 4:11 NIV

Here he is referring to a special kind of speaking, not merely teaching. Someone who gives a teaching is not usually considered to be speaking the very words of God, as is someone who speaks under the inspiration of the Spirit through prophecy, words of knowledge, tongues or interpretation of tongues. Yet even the expression of these gifts is to be weighed or tested (see the section "Discerning Prophecy and Other Gifts" in chapter 7).

To classify the gifts, this book follows a traditional division of the nine gifts listed in 1 Corinthians 12:8–10 into three categories. There are gifts of revelation: word of wisdom, word of knowledge and discernment of spirits. There are gifts of power: faith, healings and working of miracles. And there are gifts of speech: prophecy, tongues and interpretation of tongues. This is a classic and long-standing breakdown of the gifts. We recognize, however, that it is limited and somewhat artificial.

What do we mean? Prophecy and interpretation of tongues are gifts of speech, but they also depend upon revelation; otherwise, they would be little different from some forms of teaching. The gift of faith involves revelation as well. The gifts of miracles and healing are power gifts, but they are in large part dependent on the gift of faith, and are often related to words of knowledge. The gifts frequently work in conjunction with one another. In addition, there are other spiritual gifts besides the ones Paul lists here.[7]

Misconceptions about the Gifts

Among both Catholics and Protestants, there are some widespread misconceptions about the spiritual gifts that keep people from being open to them. In the following sections, we will address these misunderstandings on both sides. (**Mary** will address the Catholic misconceptions, and **Randy** will address the Protestant misconceptions.)

Are the gifts meant to be rare? (Mary)

For many Catholics, the phrase "gifts of the Holy Spirit" immediately brings to mind the seven gifts that Catholic tradition calls the sanctifying gifts of the Spirit: wisdom, understanding, counsel, fortitude, knowledge, piety and fear of the Lord.[8] These are listed in Isaiah 11:1–3, a passage that foretells the Spirit-filled Messiah who was to come.[9] Since the Holy Spirit forms in Christians the character of Jesus the Messiah (see Romans 8:29), Catholic tradition holds that these gifts are given to every Christian through the sacraments of baptism and confirmation.[10] Because of the strong emphasis on these seven, many Catholics are not aware that there are any other gifts of the Spirit. But Catholic teaching has never *limited* the Spirit's gifts to these seven. Saint Thomas Aquinas, one of the greatest theologians in history, wrote a long treatise on the spiritual gifts in his *Summa Theologica*, in which he explains several of the gifts Paul lists in 1 Corinthians 12—including prophecy, tongues and miracles—and emphasizes their importance for evangelization.[11]

Even when Catholics acknowledge the existence of the 1 Corinthians gifts, they may still think of them as very rare graces that we see in the lives of some great saints, but which ordinary folks should neither expect nor seek. This view is partly due to an imbalance that crept into theology over the centuries. Although charisms never disappeared from the life of the Catholic Church, for a long time they were neglected in both theology and practice.[12] If theologians mentioned the spiritual gifts at all, they viewed them as private endowments, given by God for the benefit of the individual but not having any importance or value for the Church. Gifts like prophecy, visions, words of knowledge and healing were viewed as extraordinary mystical phenomena that occur only in the lives of unusually prayerful people. They were not seen as necessary to the life or mission of the Church.

But this was a category mistake. In fact, charisms are not gifts for personal spiritual enrichment, but for the building up of the Body of Christ. In theological terms, they do not belong primarily under the heading of *mystical theology*, but rather of *ecclesiology* (understanding of the Church). As Catholic teaching has strongly reaffirmed since Vatican Council II, charisms are not only legitimate, but also structurally necessary to the Church. The Church has two complementary dimensions: the charismatic and the institutional. The charismatic is the Holy Spirit's distribution of charisms among all the faithful, at His own initiative, and the institutional is the Church's hierarchical leadership structure. As Pope John Paul II affirmed, these two dimensions are "co-essential" to the very nature of the Church. Both are ways that the Holy Spirit is at work in the Church.[13] Neither Scripture nor the teaching of the Catholic Church gives any grounds for thinking that the spiritual gifts should be rare.

Is it spiritually dangerous to seek the gifts? (Mary)

Another source of misunderstanding is that many Catholics have heard that seeking spiritual gifts is risky. Some may call to mind the warnings of saints and spiritual writers to be wary of supernatural manifestations since such manifestations might lead to pride, or we might be deceived by the devil, or we might begin to focus on experiences of God rather than God Himself. The sixteenth-century Carmelite monk Saint John of the Cross, for example, points out these dangers in his classic work *The Ascent of Mount Carmel*.[14] These warnings contribute to a sense among Catholics that pursuing spiritual gifts is not quite safe.

There is a vast difference, however, between a caution against the misuse of God's gifts and an outright rejection of those gifts. Ralph Martin, who has written and taught extensively on the spiritual masters of the Catholic tradition, points out that it is a mistake to think Saint John rejects the spiritual gifts:

> John is motivated not by a desire to "squelch" the charismatic gifts of the Spirit but to assure their authentic exercise. . . .
>
> Does John of the Cross condemn the exercise of the charismatic gifts? No, he doesn't. On the contrary, he gives much helpful advice about how they should be exercised so they effectively accomplish the purpose for which God gives them.[15]

John in fact reaffirms the biblical teaching that God gives these gifts so they may be used for the good of others.[16] He describes two kinds of benefits of the gifts:

> The temporal [benefit] includes healing the sick, restoring sight to the blind, raising the dead, expelling devils, prophesying the future so people may be careful, and other similar things. The spiritual and eternal benefit is the knowledge and love of God caused by these works either in those who perform them or in those in whom, or before whom, they are accomplished.[17]

At the same time, John cautions against using the gifts for any motives other than the glory of God and the good of souls. Our deepest concern, he says, must be whether the people we minister to are being converted to Christ and drawn to deeper union with Him. In giving these warnings, John is echoing Paul's teaching in Scripture that the gifts have absolutely no value apart from love (see 1 Corinthians 13).

So is it dangerous to seek the gifts? Only if one is doing so for hidden motives of pride or personal gain. It is indeed possible to use the charisms and yet not be in right relationship with God. Jesus warned that on the last day, "Many will say to me, 'Lord, Lord, did we not prophesy in your name, and cast out demons in your name, and do many mighty works in your name?' And then will I declare to them, 'I never knew you; depart from me, you workers of lawlessness'" (Matthew 7:22–23). On the other hand, because God gives the gifts so we can be conduits of His love for others, to choose *not* to seek the gifts can be a failure of love. Saint Paul exhorts us, "Pursue love, and earnestly desire the spiritual gifts" (1 Corinthians 14:1).

What gifts are available to Christians today? (Randy)

From its inception, the Protestant movement was suspicious of some of the gifts. The Lutherans and Calvinists believed that certain gifts had *ceased*, those being gifts of healings, working of miracles, tongues and interpretation of tongues. Prophecy was for all intents and purposes also denied, in that it was reinterpreted to mean simply preaching. This was the predominant Protestant view from 1517 until the birth of the Pentecostal movement in 1901.

In the mid-nineteenth century there was a major resurgence of healing within Protestantism, which continued among the Methodist, Presbyterian, Baptist and Dutch Reformed churches. The key leaders of the Faith Cure movement came from these denominations. Healing became one of the most controversial subjects—if not the most controversial—among Protestant churches by the last quarter of the nineteenth century. Thus, healing was rediscovered within Protestantism even prior to the birth of Pentecostalism. It was not so much the *gift* of healing that was emphasized, however, as it was God's healing in response to prayers of faith of the sick person, or the people or congregation praying for the sick person. Healing was connected to the promises of God and was possible without the gift of healing.

With the birth of Pentecostalism, the belief that God was restoring His gifts as they were in the apostolic age came into Protestantism. This view, *continuationism*, meaning the gifts are continuing in the Church, was a major departure from *cessationism*, meaning the gifts of healing, miracles, tongues, interpretation of tongues and prophecy had ceased. The division between cessationism and continuationism still exists among Protestant churches today; however, the number of continuationists is greatly surpassing cessationists outside Europe and North America. It has been estimated that approximately 80 percent of Protestant Christians in the majority world are continuationist.

A primary reason for sixteenth-century Protestants developing a cessationist position was the Reformation itself. Catholics were using the evidence of continued healings and miracles to argue against the legitimacy of the Protestant movement. In response, the Protestants tried to undercut this authority. Protestants, like Catholics, saw miracles as evidence of correct doctrine. The argument was that since miracles proved correct doctrine, and since Protestants believed some Catholic doctrines were inconsistent with the teaching of the Bible, then the miracles must be counterfeit. These early Protestants wanted to reduce the authority for doctrine to the Bible alone. Therefore, the gifts of healing and miracles no longer existed. Those gifts ended with the death of the apostles, or (in the view of some) with the canonization of the Bible (the finalizing of the list of books that belong in the Bible). These Protestants also believed there were no longer any apostles or prophets in the Church after the death of the original twelve apostles and Paul.

Today, the continuationist camp, made up of Pentecostals, charismatics and third-wave evangelicals, has rejected this traditional Protestant view of the gifts. "Third wave" refers to evangelicals who historically had been cessationists, but who have now accepted the continuation of the gifts in the Church.

The problem with cessationism is that it fails to recognize that miracles are not *primarily* to be used as evidence of correct doctrine. Instead, they are part and parcel of the Good News, the Gospel. Signs and wonders are to accompany the proclamation of the Gospel (see Hebrews 2:4 and Mark 16:17–20, especially verse 20). As long as the Gospel is preached, therefore, signs and wonders and the gifts of the Spirit are to continue as well.

This is also very clear from 1 Corinthians 13:8–10, which teaches that the gifts will continue until "the perfect comes" (verse 10). Although some Protestants hold that the coming of "the perfect" refers to the completion of the New Testament, the great majority of biblical scholars hold that it refers to the Second Coming of Christ. This was the argument the Church used in the second century to refute the Montanists, who were claiming that after they died, the gift of prophecy would no longer continue. The Church refuted this with Paul's statement that "when the perfect comes, the imperfect will pass away" (1 Corinthians 13:10 RSV), interpreting "the perfect comes" as the Second Coming of Jesus. Hence, the gifts were to continue until the Second Coming.

That signs and wonders, including gifts of healing and miracles, were to be part of the Gospel is clear from Jesus' commissioning of His disciples:

And he said to them, "Go into all the world and proclaim the gospel to the whole creation. Whoever believes and is baptized will be saved, but whoever does not believe will be condemned. And these signs will accompany those who believe: in my name they will cast out demons; they will speak in new tongues; they will pick up serpents with their hands; and if they drink any deadly poison, it will not hurt them; they will lay their hands on the sick, and they will recover."

Mark 16:15–18

Paul writes of "what Christ has accomplished through me in leading the Gentiles to obey God by what I have said and done—by the power of signs and wonders, through the power of the Spirit of God. So from Jerusalem all the way around to Illyricum, I have fully proclaimed the gospel of Christ" (Romans 15:18–19 NIV). It is most interesting to note that the word *proclaimed* does not appear in the Greek text, but is inserted by translators. Literally, Paul says, "I have *fulfilled the gospel* of Christ" (or "I have filled up the gospel of Christ"). Both Jesus and Paul connect the preaching of the Gospel to signs and wonders that include gifts of healing and deliverance.

When we look at the commissioning texts in the gospels, we see the central place given to healing and deliverance. Jesus "called to him his twelve disciples and gave them authority over unclean spirits, to cast them out, and to heal every disease and every affliction" (Matthew 10:1). He then continues the commission: "And proclaim as you go, saying, 'The kingdom of heaven is at hand.' Heal the sick, raise the dead, cleanse lepers, cast out demons" (verses 7–8). The gospels of Mark and Luke report the same commissioning, including the commands to preach and to heal, which the disciples faithfully carried out (see Mark 6:7, 12–13; Luke 9:1–2, 6).

As we mentioned in the introduction, Luke not only gives us the commissioning of the twelve, but also the commissioning of the seventy (or seventy-two):

> After this the Lord appointed seventy-two others and sent them on ahead of him, two by two, into every town and place where he himself was about to go. And he said to them, ". . . Heal the sick in it and say to them, 'The kingdom of God has come near to you.'"
>
> Luke 10:1–2, 9

These two commissionings, of the twelve and of the seventy-two, help us understand how we are to interpret the Great Commission in Matthew:

> Then Jesus came to them and said, "All authority in heaven and on earth has been given to me. Therefore go and make disciples of all nations, baptizing them in the name of the Father and of the Son and of the Holy Spirit, and *teaching them to obey everything I have commanded you.* And surely I am with you always, to the very end of the age."
>
> Matthew 28:18–20 (NIV, emphasis added)

The first half of this passage has been better observed and obeyed by the Church than its second half. We have been better at evangelizing and baptizing than we have been at disciple making by teaching people to obey *everything* Jesus commanded the twelve. When we look at the commissioning of the twelve and the seventy-two, we note that Jesus commands them to heal and cast out demons. Somehow the Church over the years downplayed these priorities of the commissionings and neglected Jesus' instructions about signs and wonders effected through the gifts of the Spirit.

Were the gifts legendary embellishments? (Randy)

The duration of the gifts has not been the only point of controversy among Protestants. As mentioned already, many Protestants believe the gifts were real and operated through supernatural enablement, but they also believe that after the New Testament age, the supernatural aspect disappeared. Liberal biblical scholars, however, deny the biblical accounts of the supernatural altogether. The liberal Protestant worldview does not allow for any supernatural intervention of God, so they deny the gifts as well as the literal virgin birth, the resurrection of Jesus and His Second Coming. Liberals interpret these as either explainable by naturalistic means or as having no historical basis at all—that is, they never happened. Instead, they are seen as myths or legends written to express the early Christians' theology.

As recent biblical scholarship has shown, the idea that the signs and wonders recorded in the New Testament were legendary embellishments or myth is not based on historical evidence, but rather on a bias among scholars against the supernatural. The best biblical scholarship backs up what Christians have always believed: that these were real historical events and actions on the part of the Christians. An abundance of evidence shows that they then continued throughout the history of the Church.

Are the gifts supernatural or natural? (Randy)

Fundamentalists, conservative evangelicals, and of course Pentecostals and charismatics believe in the supernatural nature of the signs and wonders, gifts of the Spirit, miracles and healings recorded in the Bible. But when it comes to the operation of the gifts today, there is disagreement regarding three gifts in particular: prophecy, word of knowledge and word of wisdom. Pentecostals and charismatics understand these gifts in a more supernatural manner, while other Protestants, both fundamentalists and liberals, understand them in a more naturalistic manner.

Fundamentalists and liberals interpret the gift of prophecy to refer to preaching or teaching. New Testament usage, however, shows that there is a distinction between prophecy, on the one hand, and preaching and teaching, on the other. Both preaching and teaching usually involve a prepared and planned message (see Acts 5:42; 1 Timothy 4:13; 5:17), whereas prophecy involves a spontaneous word spoken under the inspiration of the Holy Spirit (see Acts 19:6, 21:9–11; 1 Corinthians 14:29–32). There is no basis for thinking that this distinction has disappeared. To prophesy is to give a message to a person or group that will comfort, build up, warn or encourage the them. But this message is not based on a natural ability. No, prophecy is more. It may include bringing the message to someone who, in the natural, you did not realize needed to be encouraged, edified or comforted. Or it may be a message that has a supernatural ability to convey exactly what the person needs to hear. It is also possible for a prophecy to be directive or predictive.

Liberal Protestants, however, reject the possibility of predictive prophecy. Fundamentalists inconsistently believe that biblical prophecy can be predictive, but that prophecy exercised in the Church after the New Testament period no longer has this predictive element.

The gift of the word of knowledge is often interpreted in a similar way. For non-Pentecostals and non-charismatics, the word of knowledge refers to the ability to understand Christian doctrine, apply the principles of the Bible to the problems of daily life, teach the Christian faith and interpret the Bible. This interpretation leans much more on natural ability than on supernatural ability. It depends on human learning and intelligence rather than on God's grace giving people access to information they could not have known naturally. But the New Testament records many instances of Christians having access to such supernatural knowledge (see Acts 5:3; 9:8–12; 14:9–10; 1 Corinthians 14:24–25), by which God reveals His will in a particular setting or a specific condition that He desires to heal. This knowledge then causes a greater measure of faith to be manifest, which in turn releases gifts of power—healings and the working of miracles.

The gift of word of wisdom has likewise been interpreted as wisdom gained through experience and knowledge, rather than divine wisdom given supernaturally in the moment. For Pentecostals and charismatics, on the other hand, the word of wisdom is a supernatural leading of the Holy Spirit that gives a person wisdom in making decisions.

Having said this, it is important to understand the emphasis that must be placed on being immersed in the Word in order to exercise prophecy and other revelatory gifts. Those who consider themselves prophets (as opposed to prophesying only occasionally) must be deeply grounded in the Bible, which is the measure by which prophecies should be weighed. It is the source book for understanding the mind and ways of God. The Bible often provides language that the Holy Spirit can use to bring forth a "now" word for a person or group in the present.

How many gifts can a person have? (Randy)

Within Protestantism the teaching that each Christian has only one gift is quite popular. Each believer is to discover what his or her gift is and utilize it for the benefit of the local church. There is also a tendency for much of Protestantism to focus on the gifts of Romans 12 rather than the gifts of 1 Corinthians 12. Yet these two lists of gifts are not mutually exclusive, but complementary.

The problem with the idea that every Christian has only one gift is that the Bible teaches that Christians can operate in more than one of the gifts. Perhaps it is because of the focus on Romans 12 instead of 1 Corinthians 12 that the wrong emphasis has developed. In the popular New International Version, Romans 12:6 speaks of "your gift." The Greek does not say this, however, and it is not in most translations. In the same version, there are other verses that speak of the possibility of a Christian having more than one gift. For example, Paul says, "But earnestly desire the higher gifts," and also, "Pursue love, and earnestly desire the spiritual gifts, especially that you may prophesy" (1 Corinthians 12:31; 14:1). These two verses state that we are to desire gifts of the Spirit, especially prophecy. This indicates that although God gives the gifts as He wills, we can receive them through earnestly desiring them. Paul also tells the Corinthians that he would like for them all to speak in tongues and to desire to interpret tongues (see 1 Corinthians 14:5, 13). This again indicates the possibility of having more than one gift.

When I first was exposed to the operation of the gifts of the Spirit in an experiential way, I was talking with my wife, DeAnne, and a couple of our close friends and leaders in the Baptist church I was pastoring. We were talking about what gift we would like to have. We each named the gift we would like to move in. When we came to my wife, DeAnne said, "I want them all." Biblically speaking, she intuitively was more correct than the rest of us, who were still in the old paradigm of having only one gift.

It is also important to realize that sometimes it is when the gifts are operating together that they have the greatest impact. For example, the gifts of word of knowledge and healing often work together, causing more healings to occur. The gift of faith works with the gift of working of miracles. The gift of prophecy works with the gift of discerning of spirits. The gift of tongues works with the gift of interpretation of tongues. And the gift of word of wisdom can work with any of these gifts.

Does operating in gifts require baptism in the Spirit? (Randy)

Among Protestants who do believe that gifts of the Spirit are still operative in our time, there are three main views. First, some hold the view that the gifts do not become operative in a Christian's life until after baptism in the Holy Spirit (see chapter 4 for an explanation of baptism in the Spirit). Second, some hold that the gifts are made available to every Christian at the moment of regeneration; that is, new birth in Christ, which (for this group) is the same time that one is baptized in the Holy Spirit. Third, some hold that an individual can have access to and move in the gifts of the Spirit prior to the baptism in the Spirit, which is usually subsequent to regeneration, but that the baptism in the Spirit heightens or intensifies the gifts. This latter position was my experience, and I believe it has the greatest number of biblical texts to support it. It is not the only position, however. There are also biblical texts, though not as many, supporting the view of the baptism of the Spirit occurring simultaneously with regeneration.

How, then, do we answer the question, "Do you have to be baptized in the Holy Spirit in order to operate in the gifts?" The answer is no. One can move in the gifts of the Spirit from the moment of regeneration. It is a fact that from that moment, the Holy Spirit is in the believer: "If anyone does not have the Spirit of Christ, they do not belong to Christ" (Romans 8:9). Paul clearly states that Christians have the Spirit of Christ. If the Spirit is within us, then the potential of moving in His gifts is also within us. At the same time, it is true that there is a difference between the life of the Spirit in us in regeneration, and the power of the Spirit coming upon us in the baptism in the Spirit. With the baptism in the Spirit, or even a subsequent baptism in the Spirit—I do believe it is a repeatable experience—there is a greater anointing for moving in the gifts of the Spirit. And sometimes the baptism in the Spirit is the occasion for an impartation of a new gift.

There are many people who have received with an impartation of the Holy Spirit a gift or gifts that caused them to step into a powerful new realm of the activity of the Spirit. This experience enables them to see many more words of knowledge, healings and miracles. For others, it is the release of a greater gift of prophecy, and for still others the discerning of spirits. For some, it is tongues and interpretation of tongues; for others there is a release into all these gifts.

Mighty Deeds in Jesus' Name (Randy)

I know three people who, as a result of their impartation of greater gifts, have each led over a million people to Jesus through their ministries: Heidi Baker in Mozambique, Henry Madava in Ukraine and Leif Hetland in the Middle East.[18] That is amazing! Three people touched by the Holy Spirit led three million people to Jesus, and through Him to the Father. Three million people found God.[19]

The amazing thing is that these mighty deeds are being done in Jesus' name, regardless of whether the person is Catholic, Episcopalian, Lutheran, Baptist, Pentecostal, charismatic, Nazarene or any other Christian denomination. According to the Bible, God is looking for people through whom He can show Himself strong (see 2 Chronicles 16:9 NKJV). God is looking for people through whom He will answer Jesus' prayer in John 15:8—people who will bring the Father glory by bearing supernatural fruit done by the power of the Holy Spirit.

Though it is true that there are many God-loving Christians who do not know or believe that operating in the supernatural gifts is possible today, the good news is that the good news is spreading about who we are in Christ and what we can do in His name. The number of Christians in the world who believe in and experience the gifts of the Holy Spirit has seen explosive growth in the last century, especially in the last half century.

I long to see all God's children prophesying. I long to see the heartbeat of Christians resounding to the motto of the Moravians, that greatest of all missionary groups of eighteenth-century Protestants: "To win for the Lamb who was slain the rewards of his suffering!" Those rewards are not limited to salvation, but extend to healing and deliverance, miracles, and signs and wonders. Primarily through these God has confirmed the preaching of His Gospel. The Gospel of the Kingdom is the Gospel that the New Covenant has come. It was ratified by Jesus' blood shed at the cross, but it was enacted on the Day of Pentecost, with the outpouring of the Holy Spirit upon the Church. It continues to be Good News because of the power of God's grace made available to all through the gifts of the Spirit.

2

The Spirit of the Lord Is upon Me

The prophet Isaiah foretold that one day the Messiah would come, and the way He would be known would be by the Spirit of God resting on Him, empowering Him to do mighty deeds of healing and deliverance:

> The Spirit of the Lord GOD is upon me,
>   because the LORD has anointed me
> to bring good news to the poor;
>   he has sent me to bind up the brokenhearted,
> to proclaim liberty to the captives,
>   and the opening of the prison to those who are
>   bound;
> to proclaim the year of the LORD's favor,
>   and the day of vengeance of our God;
> to comfort all who mourn;
>   to grant to those who mourn in Zion—

> to give them a beautiful headdress instead of ashes,
>> the oil of gladness instead of mourning,
>> the garment of praise instead of a faint spirit.
>
> Isaiah 61:1–3

The Messianic age was to be an age when God's power would be released on earth, saving people from all the tragic consequences of the Fall, resulting in uncontainable joy and gladness:

> Then the eyes of the blind shall be opened,
>> and the ears of the deaf unstopped;
>> then shall the lame man leap like a deer,
>> and the tongue of the mute sing for joy.
>
> Isaiah 35:5–6

From the very beginning of Jesus' mission, the gospels show these prophecies being fulfilled, first in Him and then in His disciples.

The Pentecost Preview

Even before Jesus began His public ministry, in the events surrounding His birth, already the marvelous works of God began to be manifest through the power of the Holy Spirit. In the first chapter of Luke, the angel Gabriel comes to the virgin Mary to announce the good news that God's promises are now being fulfilled. The long-awaited Messiah, the Son of God, is coming into the world to reign as King forever, and He will be born of her. Gabriel tells Mary, "The Holy Spirit will come upon you, and the power of the Most High will overshadow you; therefore the child to be born will be called holy—the Son of God" (Luke 1:35).

These words are strikingly similar to Jesus' promise to His apostles some 34 years later, at the beginning of Acts: "You will receive power when the Holy Spirit has come upon you, and you will be my witnesses in Jerusalem and in all Judea and Samaria, and to the end of the earth" (Acts 1:8).

What happens to Mary at the incarnation is a foreshadowing of what will happen to the whole Church when the Holy Spirit is poured out on Pentecost. The incarnation is a kind of Pentecost preview. As the Holy Spirit comes powerfully upon Mary, with the result that Christ becomes present in her and she brings Him forth into the world, so the Holy Spirit will come powerfully upon the disciples at Pentecost, with the result that Christ will become present in them, so they can bring Him forth into the world through their proclamation of the Gospel.

"Behold, I am the servant of the Lord," Mary answers the angel. "Let it be to me according to your word" (Luke 1:38). The Greek term used for "let it be" indicates not just acceptance, but enthusiastic desire; a better translation is "*may it be.*" It expresses Mary's joy at the greatest news anyone has ever heard: The Messiah will be present within her! She embraces God's plan with her whole being.

Luke then shows Mary's immediate response to the Holy Spirit coming upon her: Christ is in her, and she cannot keep Him to herself. She has to share Him! So she goes "in haste" to visit her cousin Elizabeth and spread the good news.[1] Mary's visit to Elizabeth is, in fact, the very first Christian mission, the first time someone goes out to share the good news of Jesus. It sets the pattern for the Church. Just as will happen at Pentecost, the immediate effect of being filled with the Holy Spirit is evangelism.

When Mary enters the house, Elizabeth hears her voice—only a greeting, not an eloquent preaching of the Gospel or an exposition of doctrine, just a greeting from a heart overflowing with the Spirit—and the flame of the Holy Spirit seems to leap from Mary to Elizabeth, and then to the infant John in her womb. Now they, too, are filled with the Spirit and with Messianic joy.

Another immediate effect of the presence of the Holy Spirit is overflowing praise—again, just as will occur at Pentecost. Elizabeth blesses Mary for her faith and expresses wonder at this visitation of the Messiah: "And why is this granted to me that the mother of my Lord should come to me?" (Luke 1:43). Then Mary praises God in her song of praise: "My soul magnifies the Lord, and my spirit rejoices in God my Savior" (verses 46–47).

Gifts at the Dawn of Salvation

Luke even hints at other spiritual gifts in these scenes at the beginning of his gospel, gifts that the Spirit-filled disciples in Acts will later manifest after Pentecost. At the dawn of salvation, the charisms that Paul lists in 1 Corinthians 12:8–10 are already being manifested:

- Words of wisdom: Both Mary and Elizabeth speak with wisdom about God's plan of salvation (see Luke 1:42–45, 48–55).
- Words of knowledge: Before Mary sees Elizabeth, she knows supernaturally, through the message of the angel, that Elizabeth is pregnant, and Elizabeth somehow knows that Mary is the mother of the Lord (see 1:36, 43).

- Faith: Mary believes the word spoken to her by the Lord (see 1:45).

- Healing: Elizabeth and Zechariah are healed of infertility (see 1:36).

- Miracles: The Son of God becomes Man, the greatest miracle in history up to this point (see 1:35).

- Prophecy: Mary prophesies, "From now on all generations will call me blessed; for he who is mighty has done great things for me, and holy is his name" (1:48–49). Later, after the birth of John, Zechariah also prophesies: "You, child, will be called the prophet of the Most High; for you will go before the Lord to prepare his ways, to give knowledge of salvation to his people in the forgiveness of their sins" (1:76–77). When Jesus is presented in the Temple, Simeon and Anna prophesy (see 2:34–38).

- Discernment of spirits: Mary discerns that Gabriel is an angel of God, and that it is truly the Holy Spirit of God who has overshadowed her.

- Interpretation of tongues: John, a preborn baby who knows no language, hears Mary's greeting and rightly interprets what it means: God is in the room! He leaps for joy at the hidden presence of the Savior (see 1:41).

- Tongues: At the birth of John, Zechariah's "mouth was opened and his tongue was loosed" to bless the Lord, and he, too, was "filled with the Holy Spirit" (1:64, 67). Although this statement is not literally referring to the gift of tongues, it is describing a similar phenomenon: the Holy Spirit making a person bubble over with joyful praise of God.

What we learn from these scenes Luke so carefully narrated is that before evangelism is about words, or about acts of loving service, it is about the Word of God Himself, Jesus, present within us through the Holy Spirit. Evangelism is not first and foremost a matter of strategies, plans and projects, but rather of being filled with the Holy Spirit and allowing that divine life within us to burst forth in both word and action.

Jesus' Baptism in the Spirit

Thirty years later, in Jesus' public ministry, the power and gifts of the Holy Spirit became manifest again. It began when Jesus Himself was filled with the Holy Spirit at His baptism in the Jordan River.

John the Baptist had appeared in the desert, calling the people to repentance and baptizing them as a sign of cleansing from sin. John did not seek to draw attention to himself, but to the One who was to come. He cried out, "I baptize you with water, but he who is mightier than I is coming, the strap of whose sandals I am not worthy to untie. He will baptize you with the Holy Spirit and fire" (Luke 3:16).

The meaning of the word *baptize* is a key to understanding John's message. Long before it became a Christian word, *baptizō* was an ordinary Greek word. It meant "to plunge into water, immerse, soak, drench." To his contemporaries, the title John the Baptist literally meant "John the Plunger." His message was, in effect, "I am plunging you into the Jordan River as a sign of repentance, but this is only a preparation for the far greater immersion the Messiah will give you. He's going to plunge you into the Holy Spirit. He's going to inundate you with the very life of God!"

John was surprised when Jesus Himself came to be baptized (see Matthew 3:14). As the Son of God, Jesus was sinless; He did not need to repent for anything. Why, then, did He undergo John's baptism? It was Jesus' way of totally accepting the Father's plan: that He would be counted among sinners and would bear the penalty for sin. In humility, Jesus chose to be in complete solidarity with sinners, knowing that His decision would ultimately lead to the cross.

As soon as Jesus came up from the water, the Holy Spirit descended on Him "in bodily form, like a dove" (Luke 3:22). It was the moment of Jesus' baptism in the Holy Spirit. He would baptize people in the Spirit because He Himself had been baptized in the Spirit. At the same moment, God's voice was heard from heaven: "You are my beloved Son; with you I am well pleased." The essence of baptism in the Holy Spirit is to have the love of God the Father poured into one's heart by the Holy Spirit (see Romans 5:5). As the eternal Son of God, Jesus was already united with the Father, but as a man, at that moment He let His human heart be filled with the Father's love in a way that grounded His whole identity.

It was from the time of His baptism on—not before—that Jesus began to minister in power. The gospel of Luke tells us that after His baptism, Jesus was "full of the Holy Spirit" (Luke 4:1). Curiously, the first thing the Holy Spirit did was to lead Him into the desert to be tempted by the devil. Why would the Spirit lead Jesus to be tempted? Wouldn't it be more logical to lead Him away from the devil? The Spirit did this so that Jesus could be the model for all of His followers. To be led by the Holy Spirit means we have to resist those evil spirits that seek to deflect us from our God-given mission. And in the Holy Spirit, we have a God-given authority to defeat the enemy and break his influence. The temptations in the desert were only the beginning of Jesus' campaign against Satan. His whole mission was a work of dismantling the kingdom of darkness and liberating those who had been captive to it.

Significantly, the first thing the devil said to Jesus was, "*If you are the Son of God . . .*" (Luke 4:3, emphasis added). Yet just a short time earlier God had said, "*You are my beloved Son*" (Luke 3:22, emphasis added). Satan was seeking to undermine the very truth that God the Father had just affirmed. If he could get Jesus to doubt His identity as the beloved Son, then he could get Him to strive to prop up His own status with impressive acts of power, like turning stones to bread or jumping off the parapet of the Temple. And that, in turn, would ruin the Father's plan. Jesus would be attempting to be the Messiah of human success, applause and popularity, instead of the Messiah who would go to the cross. It is the same tactic the devil uses with all of us who are Christ's disciples. He seeks to undermine our identity so he can derail our destiny.

Jesus resisted that demonic attack not by His divine omnipotence, but in His human nature, filled with the power of the Holy Spirit. As Lawrence of Brindisi, a saint of the sixteenth century, put it:

> Christ came into the world to do battle against Satan. . . .
> He could have accomplished this by using the weapons of
> his might and coming as he will come to judge, in glory
> and majesty. . . . But so that his victory might be the more
> glorious, he willed to fight Satan in our weak flesh. It is as
> if an unarmed man, right hand bound, were to fight with
> his left hand alone against a powerful army; if he emerged
> victorious, his victory would be regarded as all the more

glorious. So Christ conquered Satan with the right hand of his divinity bound and using against him only the left hand of his weak humanity.[2]

Those temptations were only the first of many that recurred throughout Jesus' public ministry, sometimes through the mouths of people—even good people like Peter.[3] It culminated in the mockery Jesus endured on the cross (see Matthew 27:39–42). He resisted the temptations, continually refusing to use the power of the Holy Spirit for His own glory or self-preservation. The power of the Spirit was for ministering the Father's love to His people, especially the poor, the sick and the marginalized. As Jesus said in the gospel of John, "I have come down from heaven, not to do my own will but the will of him who sent me" (John 6:38). In so doing, He became the model for all His future disciples in their exercise of the gifts of the Spirit.

After Jesus resisted the temptations, He went "in the power of the Spirit" into Galilee to begin His ministry of teaching, healing and liberating the oppressed (Luke 4:14). Although He is God, He chose to live as a man, dependent on the Holy Spirit.

Jesus' Mission Statement

Jesus Himself explained this in His inaugural sermon, given in the synagogue of His hometown of Nazareth. The sermon was His "mission statement," summing up what His whole mission was about. He read from the same passage of Isaiah 61 that we quoted at the beginning of this chapter:

> He unrolled the scroll and found the place where it was written,

"The Spirit of the Lord is upon me,
  because he has anointed me
  to proclaim good news to the poor.
He has sent me to proclaim liberty to the captives
  and recovering of sight to the blind,
  to set at liberty those who are oppressed,
to proclaim the year of the Lord's favor."

And he rolled up the scroll and gave it back to the attendant
and sat down. And the eyes of all in the synagogue were fixed
on him. And he began to say to them, "Today this Scripture
has been fulfilled in your hearing."

Luke 4:17–21

Jesus understood this passage of Isaiah as a prophecy of
Himself. "The Spirit of the Lord is upon me" refers to His
baptism a few days earlier, when the Holy Spirit had come
upon Him. In the Old Testament, the kings of Israel were
anointed with oil (see 1 Samuel 16:13), but the oil with which
Jesus was anointed for His mission was the Holy Spirit. And
His mission, as He describes it here, was to go into all the
darkest places of human bondage—blindness, sickness and
oppression—to proclaim the Good News of the Kingdom
and visibly demonstrate it by setting people free. It was to
evangelize not only in words, but in deeds of power.

By applying this passage to Himself, Jesus was attribut-
ing all the activity of His public ministry—His healings,
miracles, exorcisms, preaching with authority, ushering in
the Kingdom of God in power—to the anointing of the Holy
Spirit imparted to Him in His human nature.

Just as Jesus' baptism in the Spirit was the foundation for
His whole mission, so the baptism in the Spirit His disciples
would receive would be the foundation for their mission.

Even the name *Christian* conveys this truth. As Theophilus of Antioch, a second-century father of the Church, wrote, "This is why we are called Christians [*christianoi*]: because we are anointed [*chriometha*] with the oil of God."[4] To be a "Christian" means to be an anointed one, a little Christ, empowered by the Spirit of Jesus for a mission that is modeled on that of Jesus Himself. That means that every Christian has an "Isaiah 61 mission" in the areas where God has placed us—to manifest the reality of the Kingdom, release captives, heal broken hearts, dispel negative influences and replace mourning with joy.

Jesus' Use of the Spiritual Gifts

Jesus is our model for using the gifts of the Spirit, because He Himself used them preeminently. As the medieval theologian Saint Thomas Aquinas taught, "Christ is the first and chief teacher of spiritual doctrine and faith, according to Hebrews 2:3–4. . . . Hence it is clear that all the gratuitous graces [the spiritual gifts] were most excellently in Christ, as in the first and chief teacher of the faith."[5]

Let's look at some of the ways Jesus manifested the gifts of the Spirit in His ministry. The most obvious were healings and miracles, but He used other gifts as well. In every case, the gifts were powerfully effective for His preaching of the Kingdom and for bringing people to faith in Him.

Word of knowledge

The gift of a word of knowledge is evident in Jesus' conversation with the Samaritan woman at the well (see John 4). Jesus was sitting by the well when the woman came to carry out her daily task of drawing water. He engaged her in conversation and offered her "living water" that would satisfy her deepest thirst. She was curious, but a bit skeptical. She challenged Him: "Sir, you have nothing to draw water with, and the well is deep. Where do you get that living water? Are you greater than our father Jacob? He gave us the well" (John 4:11–12).

Jesus explained that the water He offered her was a spring of water welling up to eternal life, but she did not fully understand Him. She thought He was offering some hidden source of running water. At this point, Jesus brought the conversation to a whole new level by revealing facts that He could not have known naturally:

> Jesus said to her, "Go, call your husband, and come here." The woman answered him, "I have no husband." Jesus said to her, "You are right in saying, 'I have no husband'; for you have had five husbands, and the one you now have is not your husband. What you have said is true."
>
> John 4:16–18

We can imagine this woman staggering back in surprise. Jesus had just exposed an area of sin and woundedness in her life that she had probably spent a lot of energy trying to hide. Her life had been a series of broken relationships and repeated rejections. She had been unfaithful to God's plan for marriage. Yet looking into Jesus' face, she saw no condemnation, only a depth of love and mercy she had never experienced before. He is the Divine Physician, and He exposes a wound only in order to heal it.

Jesus' word of knowledge, given with gentleness and respect, was what was needed to open the woman's heart.

She now realized that she was with no ordinary man: "Sir, I perceive that you are a prophet. . . . I know that Messiah is coming (he who is called Christ). When he comes, he will tell us all things" (John 4:19, 25).

By this point her heart was open enough to receive Jesus' revelation of His true identity. He answered her, "I who speak to you am he" (verse 26).

She now realized that she was in the presence of the Messiah and Lord Himself. She forgot all about her water jar, because she had now drunk of the living water—that water that this gospel later tells us is nothing other than the Holy Spirit (see John 7:37–39). She ran back to her village, exclaiming to everyone who would listen, "Come, see a man who told me all that I ever did. Can this be the Christ?" (John 4:29).

Her message was obviously incomplete; it was neither eloquent nor theologically sophisticated. Yet it was spectacularly effective. So powerful was her testimony that, as a result, the entire town came to faith in Jesus. What convinced people was the transformation and joy in this woman's face, which was evident to everyone who saw her. This formerly isolated, outcast person was now forgiven, healed, reconciled to God and filled with a living water that overflowed in her.

Another example of Jesus using a word of knowledge was when some tax collectors asked Him if He paid the Temple tax. He affirmed that He did, and then He gave Peter a lesson in living by God's providence: "Go to the sea and cast a hook and take the first fish that comes up, and when you open its mouth you will find a shekel. Take that and give it to them for me and for yourself" (Matthew 17:27). Jesus knew by a supernatural revelation of the Spirit that the shekel would be in that fish's mouth.

Prophecy

One of the earliest labels that people gave Jesus during His ministry was "the prophet." When people asked who He was, the crowds answered, "This is the prophet Jesus, from Nazareth of Galilee" (Matthew 21:11).[6] In Israel's history, a prophet was someone who not only spoke a message from God, but also performed signs that got people's attention and reinforced the verbal message. The classic biblical prophet was Elijah, who spoke God's word, caused a drought, raised the dead, parted the Jordan River and brought down fire from heaven. So it was natural for the people to see Jesus as a prophet. This label was accurate, since He, too, called Himself a prophet (see Luke 4:24; 13:33). But it was incomplete, since He is more than a prophet. He not only communicates the word of God; He *is* the very Word of God, the fullness of all God has to say to the human race.

In one sense everything Jesus said was prophetic, since His every word was from God. But on several occasions, He used the gift of prophecy in the more specific sense of foretelling what was to come—sometimes for consolation and encouragement, sometimes for warning.

Some of Jesus' prophecies about the Kingdom of God were truly astounding. He told this parable:

> The kingdom of heaven is like a grain of mustard seed that a man took and sowed in his field. It is the smallest of all seeds, but when it has grown it is larger than all the garden plants and becomes a tree, so that the birds of the air come and make nests in its branches.
>
> Matthew 13:31–32

Viewed against the backdrop of first-century geopolitics, this prophecy could seem preposterous. Jesus was a carpenter from a backwater village in the province of Galilee, who had founded a tiny movement of negligible significance. He did heal the sick and draw crowds, but those were hardly matters on the radar of the center of political power, imperial Rome. Yet Jesus prophesied that this little movement would grow far beyond the borders of Palestine, to impact the entire world: "And people will come from east and west, and from north and south, and recline at table in the kingdom of God" (Luke 13:29).

Some of His listeners may have scoffed at Jesus' seemingly grandiose claims. Yet His word has proved true. Today, more than two billion people, from every nation of the world, believe in Jesus as Savior and Lord. At times when the early Church was beleaguered and its very existence threatened by persecution, the Christians must have been encouraged by remembering His words.

Jesus also gave some prophecies of ominous warning. When His disciples were commenting on the beauty of the Jerusalem Temple, He threw what must have felt like a dash of cold water: "Do you see these great buildings? There will not be left here one stone upon another that will not be thrown down" (Mark 13:2). He went on to foretell wars, earthquakes, famines, false messiahs, the persecution of Christians, betrayal by family members and horrendous sacrilege. Although this was a prophecy of severe judgment, it was given in love, to call God's people to repentance and to prepare them for the difficult days ahead. His words were fulfilled to the letter during the next several decades, culminating in the catastrophe of AD 70, when the

Roman armies destroyed Jerusalem and burned the Temple to the ground. Part of Jesus' prophecy was a very specific instruction:

> But when you see Jerusalem surrounded by armies, then know that its desolation has come near. Then let those who are in Judea flee to the mountains, and let those who are inside the city depart, and let not those who are out in the country enter it.

> Luke 21:20–21

According to the fourth-century church historian Eusebius, the early Christians took Jesus' words very seriously and did, in fact, flee when the Roman armies approached, migrating across the Jordan River to Pella. For this reason they escaped the massive slaughter of AD 70.

Some of Jesus' prophecies were cryptic. He said to the crowds, "Truly, I say to you, there are some standing here who will not taste death until they see the kingdom of God after it has come with power" (Mark 9:1). At first glance, this might seem to be a failed prophecy. Some scholars have taken it as evidence that Jesus was mistaken, thinking His Second Coming would occur within a few short days or years. But such a conclusion is actually based on a misinterpretation of Jesus' statement. He was not referring to the full manifestation of the Kingdom at the end of history, when He will come again in glory. Rather, He was referring to the coming of the Kingdom *into* history, beginning with His resurrection and the outpouring of the Holy Spirit at Pentecost. And indeed, the Kingdom did come with power! Within a few short months after His resurrection, thousands of people were coming to believe in Jesus as Lord and to live in the peace and joy of God's kingship. The presence of the Kingdom was being powerfully manifested in the Church. The disciples were doing signs and wonders in His name, people were being set free from demons and disease, and the Gospel was being proclaimed throughout the known world.[7] Many of those who originally heard Jesus' prophecy did indeed "see" this powerful coming of the Kingdom long before they tasted death.

This example illustrates the fact that a prophecy is one thing, and its accurate interpretation is another. A prophecy about the future can only be fully understood in hindsight, since its fulfillment may look different from the way we expected. Its purpose is not to give us a detailed timetable of future events, but to prepare us so that when the prophesied event unfolds, we can be encouraged, knowing that God is truly in control and working all things according to His perfect plan. Jesus foretold the future to His disciples for this purpose. When He predicted His passion, "they did not understand this saying, and it was concealed from them, so that they might not perceive it" (Luke 9:45). But afterward, they understood (cf. John 12:16).

Jesus sometimes gave a specific prophetic word to an individual. At the Last Supper, as Peter was boasting about his determination to stay loyal to Jesus even if everyone else fell away, Jesus put a damper on his enthusiasm: "Truly, I tell you, this very night, before the rooster crows, you will deny me three times" (Matthew 26:34). Even then, Peter was more convinced of his own fortitude than of Jesus' prophetic foreknowledge, so he immediately rejected the prophecy: "Even if I must die with you, I will not deny you!" (verse 35). But within a few short hours, Jesus' word was fulfilled.

After His resurrection, Jesus took Peter aside for a walk and a private conversation. Three times He asked Peter to reaffirm his love for Him, giving Peter the chance to reverse his three denials. Then, knowing that the leader of the apostles would need to be prepared for the severe trials that lay ahead, Jesus prophesied, "Truly, truly, I say to you, when you were young, you used to dress yourself and walk wherever you wanted, but when you are old, you will stretch out your hands, and another will dress you and carry you where you do not want to go" (John 21:18–19). Some thirty years later, according to ancient Christian testimony, Peter died a martyr's death in Rome. He did "stretch out his hands" and was nailed to a cross upside down.

Why did Jesus reveal both of these painful truths to Peter beforehand? In His infinite wisdom, the Lord knows what we need to know. It is possible that without Jesus' tip-off about his denials, Peter would have been so overwhelmed by shame and guilt that he would have despaired of ever being restored to a relationship with Jesus. It is possible that without the prophecy of his martyrdom, Peter would have been tempted to avoid persecution by watering down his preaching of the Gospel, or by running away and leaving his fellow Christians to fend for themselves.

Other gifts

The gospels show Jesus using a great variety of other gifts. On His way into Jerusalem, Jesus cursed a fig tree because He found no fruit on it. The fig tree was a symbol of Israel, and the fruit represented the response of faith and love that the Lord sought from His people. The disciples were amazed to see that the tree immediately withered. Jesus said to them,

Truly, I say to you, if you have faith and do not doubt, you will not only do what has been done to the fig tree, but even if you say to this mountain, 'Be taken up and thrown into the sea,' it will happen. And whatever you ask in prayer, you will receive, if you have faith.

Matthew 21:21–22

The withering of the fig tree is an instance of the gift of faith.

The gospels are filled with accounts of Jesus' healings and casting out of demons. The healings were in a particular way the signs that confirmed Jesus' identity as Messiah. When John the Baptist was thrown into prison, he began to have doubts about God's plan, and he sent messengers to ask Jesus if He really was the Messiah.

When the men had come to him, they said, "John the Baptist has sent us to you, saying, 'Are you the one who is to come, or shall we look for another?'" In that hour he healed many people of diseases and plagues and evil spirits, and on many who were blind he bestowed sight. And he answered them, "Go and tell John what you have seen and heard: the blind receive their sight, the lame walk, lepers are cleansed, and the deaf hear, the dead are raised up, the poor have good news preached to them."

Luke 7:20–22

For all who had eyes to see, Jesus' healings were the unmistakable proof that He truly was the Messiah, the Lord our Healer (see Exodus 15:26; Isaiah 35:5–6), who had come to restore human beings to the fullness of life that God intended for them.

Jesus' miracles include calming a storm on the sea, walking on water, changing water into wine, twice multiplying a few loaves and fish to feed crowds of thousands, and raising three people from the dead (the daughter of Jairus, the son of the widow of Nain, and Lazarus). The two miraculous catches of fish, when the disciples let down their nets at Jesus' word even though they had previously caught nothing, can be regarded as instances of the gift of miracles together with the word of knowledge (see Luke 5:4–6; John 21:5–11).

Jesus' discernment of spirits is evident in His casting out of demons. Sometimes, He identified the evil spirits by the harm they were causing: "You mute and deaf spirit, I command you, come out of him and never enter him again" (Mark 9:25). After the 72 disciples returned from their mission, Jesus saw into the spiritual realm and recognized what was truly occurring as the disciples delivered people from demonic bondage: "I saw Satan fall like lightning from heaven" (Luke 10:18).

Did Jesus ever speak in tongues? The gospels do not mention it explicitly, but it is possible that Luke has this gift in mind when he says Jesus "rejoiced in the Holy Spirit" and praised God (Luke 10:21). To rejoice in the Holy Spirit is not merely to be happy, but to have a supernatural joy inspired by the Holy Spirit. Throughout Acts, Luke closely links the gift of tongues with both the Holy Spirit and joyful praise of God.

Jesus used the spiritual gifts throughout His public ministry not only to manifest the presence of the Kingdom, but also to model for His disciples how to live life in the Spirit. But in order for them to live that new life and continue His mission on earth, something more was needed: They, too, needed to be plunged into ("baptized in") the Holy Spirit, just as He had been. In the next chapter, we will look at how that heavenly empowerment took place.

3

Clothed with Power

Before He ascended into heaven, Jesus gave His disciples the Great Commission, in which He assigned them the task of bringing the Gospel to the ends of the earth.[1] But there is a part of the Great Commission that has been so neglected in recent centuries that it could be called the Great Omission: "Stay in the city until you have been clothed with power from on high" (Luke 24:49). How are Christians supposed to carry out the gargantuan task of making disciples of all nations? There is only one way: by divine empowerment—by the power of the Holy Spirit and His gifts. The gifts are not ornaments for the spiritual lives of a few special people, but are the God-given equipment that enables the Church to accomplish her mission.

The early Christians took Jesus' command at face value. Both in the time of the apostles and in the age of the church fathers, it was common for ordinary believers to use extraordinary gifts. The gifts were considered the normal provisions

God gave to every baptized believer to carry out his or her evangelizing mission. Thus, the resurgence of understanding and practicing the spiritual gifts that is occurring all over the world in our time is not something novel, but is a return to normal.

Gifts of the Spirit in Acts

Let's explore what Luke says about the gifts in his second volume, the book of Acts. Luke's record reinforces what Paul says about the gifts in his epistles, although there is a difference in emphasis. Paul and Luke look at the work of the Holy Spirit through two different lenses. While Paul focuses mostly on the Holy Spirit's inner work of sanctification and His role in relation to our new life in Christ, Luke focuses mostly on the Holy Spirit's bestowing of power for ministry.[2] Our theology of the Holy Spirit is enriched when we allow both of these emphases to speak, rather than when we try to conform the Spirit's activity to only one or the other.

At the beginning of Acts, we find Jesus giving instruction to His disciples about the promised Holy Spirit (see Acts 1:4–8). The disciples are operating in their own strength, but they will receive power from the Holy Spirit to be witnesses of the Gospel, testifying to all the known world, with miracles accompanying. Their commission has been enlarged, and they will carry it out filled with courage and zeal and all the gifts necessary to accomplish the task set before them.

Jesus' promise is fulfilled soon afterward, at Pentecost, when the 120 disciples are gathered in the Upper Room in Jerusalem (see Acts 2:1–4). Some of those present—the apostles—had already received the Holy Spirit on the night of the resurrection, when Jesus breathed on them and said, "As the Father has sent me, even so I am sending you. . . . Receive the Holy Spirit" (John 20:21–22). For the others who had not been present that night, the Upper Room was their initial filling with the Spirit. The coming of the Spirit was marked by audiovisual phenomena: the sound of the blowing of a mighty wind (an audible experience), the fire that separated into what looked like tongues that came and rested on each of them (a visual experience), and the experience of speaking in languages they had not learned, as enabled by the Spirit. The overwhelming divine life and power brought by the Holy Spirit made the disciples appear as if they were drunk.

Peter addressed the crowd, explaining that the outpouring of the Spirit was the fulfillment of prophecy spoken by the prophet Joel (see Acts 2:14; Joel 2:28–32). At the end of his Pentecost sermon, Peter gave the command to repent and be baptized in order to receive the gift of the Holy Spirit. He concluded by saying that this gift is "for you and for your children and for all who are far off—everyone whom the Lord our God calls to himself" (Acts 2:39), which means it was not just for those in the first generation of the Church.

Signs and wonders

As the believers began to walk in their new life in the Holy Spirit, "awe came upon every soul, and many wonders and signs were being done through the apostles" (Acts 2:43). Today, it seems that not all of the Church has made the connection between signs and wonders and the gifts of the Holy Spirit. The gifts of faith, word of knowledge, discernment of spirits, prophecy, healing and miracles are very often the means by which signs and wonders occur.

We can see an example of the gift of faith at work in the healing of the lame man at the Beautiful Gate of the Temple (see Acts 3:1–10). Through some means of revelation—perhaps a word of knowledge or prophecy—Peter's faith was quickened by the grace of God, enabling him to believe with the gift of faith that the man would be healed. Otherwise, why hadn't Peter healed the man before, when he had passed him at the Beautiful Gate? The gift of faith brings a strong conviction of something God wants to do in the moment.

Another outpouring of the Spirit

Even though the believers were already filled with the Holy Spirit at Pentecost, Luke records an occasion soon afterward when the Holy Spirit was poured out on them again. As they were starting to experience persecution from the religious leaders, the Christians prayed, praising God for His sovereignty and power. They ended their prayer by saying, "And now, Lord, look upon their threats and grant to your servants to continue to speak your word with all boldness, while you stretch out your hand to heal, and signs and wonders are performed through the name of your holy servant Jesus" (Acts 4:29–30). The "hand" of God is a Jewish expression for God's manifest power. After they prayed, "the place in which they were gathered together was shaken, and they were all filled with the Holy Spirit and continued to speak the word of God with boldness" (verse 31).

God answered both of their petitions: He made them bold, and He granted them signs and wonders by stretching out His hand to release His gifts of power. This is one of the most important prayer meetings and outpourings of the Holy Spirit in the Bible, with some of the greatest fruit. The effect of that prayer—the empowerment—was something felt by the whole community of believers, apostles and laity alike, on whom the Spirit of God had fallen.

Randy: As I began to study Acts 4:29–31, I was taken with the impact of the prayer meeting, in particular how the place where they were meeting was shaken. The more I thought about this, the more a desire rose in my heart. I began to pray, telling the Lord I had seen a lot of people shake, but had never been in a meeting where the presence of God caused the building to shake. *Lord,* I said, *I would love to be in a meeting and have You shake the building just once before I die.* I was shocked when three days later, on June 3, 2017, at Dayspring Church of Castle Hills, Australia, the shaking happened. My colleague, Tom Jones, was speaking about impartation, when suddenly there was a noise, and then a shaking began. The shaking was noticeable and lasted about ten to twenty seconds. I saw people looking at each other, yet no one said anything. Later, we all began to talk among ourselves, asking each other if anyone had felt the shaking. Many had felt it all across the front of the church and on the platform. The sound technician confirmed that none of his equipment had caused the shaking, nor had there been a jet overhead, a train nearby or an earthquake. God had simply answered my prayer, and quickly.

The results of empowerment

In Acts 4 and 5 we find the apostles testifying with great power, while all the believers were ministering to the poor among them in a unity of love that resulted from the empowerment of the Holy Spirit (see Acts 4:32–35). The apostles were performing many signs and wonders, with the result that many believers were added to their number. It was the power of God accompanying the preaching of the apostles that caused the Church to grow, and this is still true today. Not only were the apostles boldly proclaiming the word, but all of those present were also empowered by being filled with the Holy Spirit, enabling them to speak the word of God boldly. The emergence of the social justice aspect of the Gospel, as seen in Acts 6:1–6, caused further growth (see verse 7).

Luke gives us a picture of the tremendous faith expressed by the crowds that gathered from around Jerusalem, bringing their sick and those tormented by evil spirits (see Acts 5:12–16). This faith must have come from hearing the testimony of others, just as occurred in Jesus' own ministry.[3] People were healed even by simply having Peter's shadow fall on them. It was not Peter's shadow that healed, but God's energy that was at work within him. It may have been people's faith regarding the gift of healing in Peter that activated their healing, or it is possible that the anointing on Peter was so strong that it extended beyond his physical body to heal people.

The connection between grace and power was demonstrated in Stephen, "full of grace and power," who "was doing great wonders and miraculous signs among the people" (Acts 6:8). Stephen preached with such great wisdom in the power of the Spirit that the glory of God was manifested through him (see verse 10).

Later, we see further fruit from the outpouring of the Spirit. Luke states that "they were all scattered throughout the regions of Judea and Samaria, except the apostles," and that "those who were scattered went about preaching the word" (Acts 8:1, 4). (They had been scattered due to persecution.) Among those scattered was Philip, who led a great evangelistic campaign in Samaria (see Acts 8:5–25). It is reasonable to believe that Stephen and Philip were present for the prayer meeting reported in Acts 4:29–31, and that they and many others were overwhelmed by the Holy Spirit and were enabled to preach the word boldly with signs and wonders, as the Church had prayed.

The lay Christians who had been scattered from Jerusalem continued to evangelize, "and a great many people were added to the Lord" (Acts 11:24). Again, the hand of the Lord was with them. It is important to note that the Church at Antioch was born through the ministry of people who were not part of the twelve apostles, but who were touched in that prayer meeting and scattered after Stephen's martyrdom. They were moving in the boldness they had prayed for, and in the signs and wonders they had prayed for.

The universality of the Gospel

One might say the evangelism in power that spread due to the Acts 4 outpouring of the Spirit was a major impetus to break the Church out beyond its Jewishness. At the beginning, the members of the Church were all Jews. The next group of people to believe in Christ was the Samaritans (descendants of the ten northern tribes of Israel) whom Philip reached in Acts 8. The next group was the Gentiles whom Peter reached at Cornelius's house. In each case, the Holy Spirit was poured out in a dramatic and perceptible way. This was a most important sign that opened the minds of the early Christians to believe that Gentiles, too, were being saved by Christ on the basis of faith. In the case of

Samaria, the Holy Spirit did not fall on the new believers until Peter and John arrived and laid hands on them, allowing the apostles themselves to witness this significant movement of the Spirit upon outsiders. God had now accepted the hated, despised Samaritans, as proven by a testimony of the Spirit so visible that even an outsider like Simon the sorcerer could see it, prompting him to try to buy this power from Peter (see Acts 8:18–24). Later, Paul's mission among the Gentiles would be received more favorably because of the evangelistic breakthroughs that occurred with Philip in Samaria and Peter in Caesarea.

When Peter came to the home of Cornelius, a Gentile centurion, he began to preach the Gospel, and before he had finished, the Holy Spirit fell upon all who heard it (see Acts 10:44–46). The fact that they received the Spirit while Peter was still delivering his sermon is significant. What was Peter saying the moment the Spirit fell? He had just said, "To him all the prophets bear witness that everyone who believes in him receives forgiveness of sins through his name" (Acts 10:43). The Holy Spirit fell upon Cornelius and his household when Peter proclaimed the universality of the Gospel—that it was for everyone, not just the Jews. The Jewish believers who had come with Peter "were amazed, because the gift of the Holy Spirit was poured out even on the Gentiles. For they were hearing them speaking in tongues and extolling God" (verses 45–46). Peter's reply shows his responsiveness to what God had done: "Can anyone withhold water for baptizing these people, who have received the Holy Spirit just as we have?" (verse 47). With this interpretation, the early Christians understood that Gentiles, too, had received God's acceptance and forgiveness, as confirmed by the witness of

His Spirit. These Gentiles were seen as being made eligible for baptism, and the evidence for this was their praising God in tongues.

This event made the apostles and the early leadership of the Church open to the Gentile mission. The leaders in Jerusalem listened as Peter explained the whole story of Cornelius and his household. Peter recounted,

> As I began to speak, the Holy Spirit fell on them just as on us at the beginning. And I remembered the word of the Lord, how he said, "John baptized with water, but you will be baptized with the Holy Spirit." If then God gave the same gift to them as he gave to us when we believed in the Lord Jesus Christ, who was I that I could stand in God's way?
>
> Acts 11:15–17

Upon hearing the story, "they fell silent. And they glorified God, saying, 'Then to the Gentiles also God has granted repentance that leads to life'" (verse 18). The apostles giving witness of the outpouring of the Spirit on different people groups solidified the unity of the Church.

From the above, it is evident that Luke does not intend to develop a standard chronology for when believers are filled with the Spirit. Neither does he attempt to create a test for determining if one has been filled or baptized with the Holy Spirit. The evidence for being Spirit-filled, according to Luke, is the receiving of power—power to serve; power to love; power to heal, deliver, or work a miracle; power to suffer persecution; power to preach the Gospel; power to comprehend the Gospel. This is seen by the diversity of experiences that Luke records.

The Spirit-anointed missions of Paul

It is interesting that the great apostle and missionary Paul was not filled with the Holy Spirit through the hands of another apostle. This was unlike what had happened in Samaria, where God used the hands of apostles to fill the Samaritans. It was also unlike the house of Cornelius, where the Spirit fell upon the Gentile God-fearers during Peter's sermon. When Paul was filled with the Spirit, God used Ananias, a disciple in Damascus. Ananias is not called an apostle or an elder or even an evangelist. He is merely called a disciple.

As the narrative progresses, it appears that Paul's evangelizing in Athens was not as successful as in other places where there was more evidence of the hand of the Lord being upon them (see Acts 17:32–34). Perhaps the meager fruit had nothing to do with Paul's sermons, but with the condition of the hearts of the listeners. His efforts in Corinth would bear more fruit. There, the Lord spoke to Paul in a vision, instructing him to keep on preaching and not be silent in the face of opposition (see Acts 18:9–11). Paul's first letter to the Corinthians indicates that there was a full demonstration of gifts of the Spirit in Corinth: "My speech and my message were not in plausible words of wisdom, but in demonstration of the Spirit and of power" (1 Corinthians 2:4). In the same letter he wrote, "For the kingdom of God does not consist in talk but in power," and he speaks of the Holy Spirit giving "the working of miracles" (1 Corinthians 4:20; 12:10).

Luke gives one more account of an outpouring of the Spirit, this time on the disciples at Ephesus in Acts 19. Again, it is through the hands of an apostle. Many biblical scholars hold that these twelve "disciples" in Ephesus were not Christians, but were disciples of John the Baptist. Since they seem to have known little of Jesus, they may not actually have heard the Baptist himself, but only some of his followers who did not preach the same message as John. (John's preaching *did* mention Jesus and the Spirit.) When Paul realized the twelve men had not received or even heard of the Holy Spirit, he explained to them that John's baptism was preparatory to believing in Jesus. Then they were baptized, receiving the new birth in Christ. But they had yet to have the Holy Spirit come upon them. It was when Paul laid his hands on them that the Spirit came upon them and they spoke in tongues and prophesied. It is clear that for Luke, when the Spirit comes on people, there is a visible manifestation. Whether it be speaking in tongues, prophesying, praising or preaching boldly, there always seems to be a verbal manifestation.

In Ephesus, as in every city he visited, Paul's pattern was to preach to Jews first, then to Gentiles. Luke makes the amazing statement that "this continued for two years, so that all the residents of Asia heard the word of the Lord, both Jews and Greeks" (Acts 19:10). If one were to ask how this could have happened in just two years, the next verses could be the answer: "And God was doing extraordinary miracles by the hands of Paul, so that even handkerchiefs or aprons that had touched his skin were carried away to the sick, and their diseases left them and the evil spirits came out of them" (verses 11–12). This is the only reference in Acts to "extraordinary" miracles, and it gives insight into the meaning of the phrase "the hand of the Lord was with them" (Acts 11:21). This great evangelistic campaign, probably the greatest in the book of Acts, was characterized by power.

Randy: These extraordinary miracles continue today. I have witnessed them personally. I have seen people with necrotic tissue and destroyed limbs be completely healed. I have seen sight be restored to an eye that had no optic nerve, and I have seen miracles where the corneas and pupils of both eyes destroyed by muriatic acid were re-created and sight was restored. I have seen stroke victims be completely healed and paranoid schizophrenia be verifiably healed. In Mozambique God has raised people from the dead, causing whole villages to turn to Jesus, believe the Gospel and receive baptism.

After two years of preaching, with signs and wonders that impacted an entire province, Paul left Ephesus and headed to Macedonia, and then later to Troas, where he raised a young man from the dead (see Acts 20:7–12). In the remainder of Acts, we find Paul continuing to travel, preach and minister in spite of opposition and attempts on his life.

The final chapter of Acts recounts two supernatural events occurring on Malta. The first occurs when a poisonous snake bites Paul. The people of the island expect him to fall over dead rather quickly, but nothing happens to him. Then Paul hears that the father of the leading man of the island is sick with fever and dysentery, so he goes to him. After praying, Paul lays hands on the man and heals him, with powerful effect: "And when this had taken place, the rest of the people on the island who had diseases also came and were cured" (Acts 28:9). This is the gift of healing in operation. Yet Paul's words in Colossians 1:29 should be kept in mind as well: "For this I toil, struggling with all his energy that he powerfully works within me." There are gifts of faith, healings, miracles, prophecy and words of knowledge, but there is also the grace of God's energy working powerfully within us.

The events on Malta are the last supernatural manifestations of the Holy Spirit mentioned in Acts. Paul reaches Rome and calls for a meeting with the Jewish leaders, some of whom are convinced by his message, but others of whom reject it. Paul again emphasizes that the Gospel will go to the Gentiles, who will accept it. Acts ends with Paul under house arrest, but he "welcomed all who came to him, proclaiming the kingdom of God and teaching about the Lord Jesus Christ with all boldness and without hindrance" (Acts 28:30–31).

One of the most insightful passages of Scripture regarding Paul's work in the area covered in Acts is found in Romans 15:15–20. Here, Paul refers to his work of proclaiming the Gospel all the way from Jerusalem around to Illyricum. This area encompasses the entire territory covered in Acts, and even beyond. Illyricum is modern-day Albania, Croatia and Serbia—all north of Greece. There is no record of this missionary journey in Acts. This means that there were more cities Paul reached than were recorded in that book. How did he go about his ministry? The answer is in verse 18: Paul sees his ministry as "what Christ has accomplished through me."

Paul led the Gentiles to faith in Christ "by the power of signs and wonders, by the power of the Spirit" (verse 19). Here we see, with even greater emphasis than in Acts, the centrality of signs and wonders and the power of the Spirit of God in the preaching of the Gospel. The grace that God gave Paul to be a minister of Christ Jesus to the Gentiles was not just undeserved election for that role, or undeserved forgiveness, but a *divine enablement to carry out the ministry of Christ in the anointing of the Holy Spirit, through the power and gifts of the Holy Spirit.* Fulfilling the Gospel is more than preaching, more than the words we speak. It is also what Christ has done through us.

Gifts in the Age of the Church Fathers

Preaching the Gospel in the power of the Holy Spirit continued during the first several centuries of the Church. During this time, Christians were in a vulnerable situation. Christianity was not legally recognized in the Roman Empire, and there were frequent outbreaks of violent persecution. Becoming a believer in Christ could cost you social ostracism, mockery, loss of employment, torture or death. And yet, it is estimated that during this same period the Church grew at the staggering rate of about 40 percent per decade.[4] By the middle of the fourth century, nearly half the population of the Roman Empire had joined the once-despised community of believers in Jesus. What explains such explosive growth?

There was a combination of factors,[5] all of them bearing the imprint of the Holy Spirit. People could see that the Christians truly loved one another. There was peace, harmony and mutual respect in their families; they did not treat women as property or expose unwanted babies to die (the ancient world's equivalent of abortion). If there was a plague in a city, the Christians cared for victims rather than fleeing for their lives like everyone else. They preached the Gospel boldly and faced martyrdom joyfully. The God they preached, the one Creator of all, was a God of steadfast love, not of cruelty and fickle passions like the pagan gods. The Lord they preached, Jesus, was a Savior who had laid down His life for us and had conquered sin and death. And besides all this, the Christians backed up their message of the Good News with demonstrations of the Holy Spirit's power, healing the sick and casting out demons.[6] It is hard to exaggerate the impact of these manifestations of God's love on the ancient pagan world. The Kingdom of God was visibly breaking in on a culture that had been mired in moral and spiritual darkness. The sun of justice was rising with its healing rays (cf. Malachi 4:2). It is no wonder that people were flocking to join the Church of Jesus, the Divine Physician.

Extraordinary works through ordinary Christians

Saint Irenaeus of Lyon (c. AD 115–202) was a third-generation Christian who as a boy had learned the Gospel from Saint Polycarp, who in turn heard it from the apostle John. Irenaeus attests to the widespread use of supernatural gifts in his time:

Those who are truly the Lord's disciples . . . perform [miracles] in his name for the well-being of others, according to the gift that each one has received from him. For some truly drive out devils, so that those who have been cleansed from evil spirits frequently believe and join the Church. Others have foreknowledge of things to come: they see visions, and utter prophecies. Still others heal the sick by laying their hands on them, and they are made whole. Yes, moreover, the dead have even been raised up, and remained among us for many years. And what more shall I say? It is not possible to name the number of the gifts that the Church throughout the whole world has received from God, in the name of Jesus Christ who was crucified under Pontius Pilate, and which she exercises day by day for the benefit of the Gentiles. . . .[7]

Irenaeus takes for granted that the use of such supernatural gifts was not rare and extraordinary, but part of the ordinary life of the Church.

As Irenaeus points out, being delivered from evil spirits was a motivating factor for many people to become Christian. Because the ancient Roman Empire was filled with demon-afflicted people, the casting out of demons was one of the gifts most in demand—as it is once again today. The Christians' ability to liberate such people was so well-known that a prominent philosopher like Saint Justin Martyr (c. AD 100–165) could use it as an argument for the truth of the Gospel. He wrote to the Senate of Rome,

> Jesus was born by the will of God the Father for the salvation of believers and the destruction of demons. And now you can learn this by what you see with your own eyes. For throughout the whole world and in your city there are many demoniacs whom all the other exorcists, sorcerers and magicians could not heal, but whom our Christians have healed and do heal, disabling and casting out the demons who possessed them in the name of Jesus Christ who was crucified under Pontius Pilate.[8]

Christians clearly had an authority over evil spirits that other exorcists sought but could not attain, because the authority came from Christ alone.

Another early writer, Origen, noted that it was usually the most ordinary Christians who expelled demons—to the greater humiliation of the demons!

> For the most part it is uneducated persons who perform this work, thus making manifest the grace that is in the word of Christ and the despicable weakness of demons, which, in

order to be overcome and driven out of the bodies and souls
of men, do not require the power and wisdom of those who
are mighty in argument or most learned in matters of faith.[9]

The simplicity of those who carried out this ministry showed
all the more clearly that the credit belonged to Christ alone.

Stirring up expectancy

In the early Church, the typical context in which a Christian began to manifest the gifts of the Spirit was baptism.[10]
Preparing for baptism was a process that sometimes took as
long as two or three years. During that time, the catechumens
(people preparing for baptism) were taught Christian doctrine and were encouraged to look forward to their baptism
with great expectancy. Since many were coming out of a life
of pagan idolatry and immorality, they were undergoing a
profound conversion. In the meantime, they were experiencing the love, acceptance and support of the Christian
community, which for many was a radically new experience.
All this preparation culminated in a powerful experience
at the Easter liturgy, in which they were immersed in the
baptismal waters, received the laying on of hands and/or an
anointing with sacred oil for the gift of the Holy Spirit, and
were allowed for first time to participate in the Eucharist,
the Lord's Supper.

One of the earliest Christian testimonies is by Saint Cyprian
of Carthage in North Africa (c. AD 200–258), who converted
as a young adult. In a letter to a friend, he gives a moving
account of what happened at his baptism:

> I went down into those life-giving waters, and all the stains of
> my past were washed away. I committed my life to the Lord;

he cleansed my heart and filled me with the Holy Spirit. I was born again, a new man. Then in a most marvelous way all my doubts cleared up. I could now see what had been hidden from me before. I found I could do things that had previously been impossible. . . .

You know as well as I do what sins I died to at that moment, just as you know the gifts the Holy Spirit gave me along with my new life. I have no desire to boast, but it is surely right to thank God for his free gift. . . . God pours out his Spirit without measure. . . . By that grace we are given power in all purity to heal the sick, whether of body or mind, to reconcile enemies, to quell violence, to calm passions, to reprimand demons and force them to disclose their identity, punishing them with sharp blows until, with loud shrieks and struggles, they flee in terror.[11]

Cyprian vividly experienced at the same time both the Holy Spirit's *sanctifying* power—a new power to resist sin and live for God—and His *charismatic* power for healing, deliverance and other gifts. Interestingly, Cyprian includes among the gifts of the Spirit the reconciliation of enemies and the quelling of violence—gifts that are also being powerfully manifested in parts of the world today.

It is striking how often the early Christian bishops and other teachers sought to stir up in the catechumens a desire for supernatural gifts. The normal expectation was that when people were newly reborn in Christ, the Holy Spirit would impart these charisms to equip them for their mission as Christ's witnesses in the world. Tertullian (c. AD 160–225), for example, exhorted the catechumens to pray for the gifts:

You blessed ones, for whom the grace of God is waiting, when you come up from the most sacred bath of the new birth, when you spread out your hands for the first time in your mother's house with your brethren, ask your Father, ask your Lord, for the special gift of his inheritance, the distributed charisms. . . . "Ask," he says, "and you shall receive."[12]

The "bath of the new birth" is baptism, and "your mother's house" is the Christian community, the Church. The "spreading out of hands" refers to standing with arms raised and palms open, the customary posture for praising God in the ancient Church, just as it is today.[13]

Saint Cyril (c. AD 318–386), bishop of Jerusalem, explained to catechumens how the Holy Spirit would pour out diverse gifts among them:

> The Holy Spirit . . . distributes his grace to each, according to his will (1 Cor 12:11). . . . For he employs the tongue of one person for wisdom; the soul of another he enlightens by prophecy; to another he gives power to drive away devils; to another he gives ability to interpret the divine Scriptures.[14]

Cyril was not content merely to impart information about the gifts. He recognized the need to awaken expectant faith for the gifts, so he urged the catechumens,

> Let each one prepare himself to receive the heavenly gift of prophecy. . . . If you believe, you will not only receive forgiveness of sins, but also do things that surpass human power. . . . My final words, beloved ones, are words of exhortation, urging all of you to prepare your souls for receiving the heavenly charisms.[15]

Another bishop, Saint Hilary of Poitiers (c. AD 300–368), explained that the gifts may be manifested in small ways at first, but they grow with use:

We who have been reborn through the sacrament of baptism experience intense joy when we feel within us the first stirrings of the Holy Spirit. We begin to have insight into the mysteries of faith; we are able to prophesy and speak with wisdom. We become steadfast in hope and receive abundant gifts of healing. Demons are made subject to our authority. These gifts enter us as a gentle rain. Little by little they bear abundant fruit.[16]

Convinced by the facts

One of the greatest theologians in history, Saint Augustine of Hippo (AD 354–430), had assumed as a young bishop that miracles and other supernatural gifts only occurred during the Church's initial stages of growth. Such charisms, he thought, had ceased after the age of the apostles. But Augustine was forced to change his mind when he witnessed so many remarkable healings in his own cathedral in Hippo that he could no longer deny that God continued to do miracles in the present. He even established the practice of recording these wonderful works of God to ensure that they would not be forgotten:

I realized how many miracles were occurring in our own day . . . and how wrong it would be to allow the memory of these miracles of divine power to perish among the people. . . . It is only two years ago that the keeping of records was begun here in Hippo, and already, at this writing, we have more than seventy attested miracles.[17]

Augustine records the details of many of these miracles in his great work *The City of God*. One that he witnessed personally involved a friend who was afflicted with horrible fistulae in his rectum. The man had already undergone one operation but needed a second. Terrified of the pain, the man prayed fervently. Augustine wrote,

> For such was the terror his former pains had produced, that he had no doubt he would die in the hands of the surgeons. . . . He began to pray; but in what a manner, with what earnestness and emotion, with what a flood of tears, with what groans and sobs, that shook his whole body, and almost prevented him speaking, who can describe! Whether the others prayed, and had not their attention wholly diverted by this conduct, I do not know. For myself, I could not pray at all. This only I briefly said in my heart: "O Lord, what prayers of your people do you hear if you do not hear these?" . . .
>
> The dreaded day dawned . . . the surgeons arrived . . . the frightful instruments are produced; all look on in wonder and suspense. While those who have most influence with the patient are cheering his fainting spirit, his limbs are arranged on the couch so as to suit the hand of the operator; the knots of the bandages are untied; the part is bared; the surgeon examines it, and, with knife in hand, eagerly looks for the sinus that is to be cut. He searches for it with his eyes; he feels for it with his finger; he applies every kind of scrutiny: he finds a perfectly firm cicatrix! No words of mine can describe the joy, and praise, and thanksgiving to the merciful and almighty God which was poured from the lips of all, with tears of gladness. Let the scene be imagined rather than described![18]

It is noteworthy that this cure, like so many others, did not involve anyone known for a particular gift of healing, just a suffering person surrounded by his friends, all praying together fervently for the Lord to heal.

Prophecy and visions

In the early centuries, prophets continued to play a vital role in the Church, as they had in the time of the apostles. The prophets included men and women, young and old, laypeople and ordained. Irenaeus speaks of the widespread use of prophecy in his time: "We hear many of the brethren in the church possessing prophetic charisms and speaking all kinds of languages through the Spirit; and bringing the secrets of men to light for their good, and expounding the mysteries of God."[19] He also mentions false prophets, but strongly warns church leaders not to make the fact that there is false prophecy a pretext for rejecting the true gift of prophecy.[20] Justin Martyr also mentions that both true and false prophets were active in the Church in his time.[21]

In third-century North Africa, Cyprian reports that even young boys had supernatural visions and that church leaders paid close attention, recognizing that the Lord was warning and instructing them through these visions.[22] Synods of bishops even heeded such prophetic messages when choosing people for church offices. For instance, a man named Celerinus was appointed to the clergy because of a prophetic revelation. Although Celerinus hesitated to accept the honor, he himself was then persuaded by a vision in the night.[23]

Tertullian describes a woman in his church who was highly regarded because of her exceptional gifts:

> We have now among us a sister who has been favored with various gifts of revelation, which she experiences in the Spirit by ecstatic vision during the sacred rites of the Lord's day in the church: she converses with angels, and sometimes even

with the Lord; she sees and hears mysterious communications; some men's hearts she understands, and to them who are in need she distributes remedies. . . . [24]

After the Sunday services, this woman would regularly convey her revelations to the clergy, who would then examine them with scrupulous care to discern whether they were in accord with truth.

Christians who were facing imminent martyrdom seem to have received especially strong prophetic graces. One of the most remarkable documents from early Christianity is the account of the martyrdom of Saint Perpetua. She was a young African noblewoman who became a believer and soon afterward was imprisoned along with four other converts, including a pregnant slave named Felicity. Perpetua's brother was distraught at the prospect of her death, and he begged her to ask the Lord for a vision showing whether she would die or escape. She confidently promised him, "Tomorrow I will tell you."

That night, she did receive a vision: She saw a golden ladder reaching up to heaven, with swords, lances, hooks and daggers along its sides. Under it a huge dragon was crouching, ready to attack whoever ascended. She saw a fellow convert named Saturus climb the ladder and then turn to her, saying, "Perpetua, I am waiting for you; but be careful not to let the dragon bite you." In her diary Perpetua further describes the dream,

> I said, "In the name of the Lord Jesus Christ, he shall not hurt me." And from under the ladder itself, as if in fear of me, [the dragon] slowly lifted up his head; and as I stepped on the first step, I stepped on his head. And I went up, and

I saw an immense garden, and in the midst of the garden a white-haired man sitting in the clothing of a shepherd, of tall stature, milking sheep; and standing around were many thousands of white-robed ones. And he raised his head and looked at me, and said, "You are welcome, daughter." And he called me, and from the cheese as he was milking he gave me a kind of little cake . . . and I ate it, and all who stood around said Amen.[25]

Perpetua awoke still tasting an indescribable sweetness. She told her brother the vision, and they understood that she would soon share in Christ's sufferings. She and her fellow Christians faced the prospect of martyrdom with such serenity that because of their witness, the jailer became a Christian, even though he knew it meant certain death.

Gifts for evangelization

It was in the context of evangelization, more than any other area of the Church's life, that spiritual gifts abounded. A layman named Gregory, who became known as the Wonderworker, "performed many miracles, healing the sick, and casting out devils . . . such that the pagans were no less attracted to the faith by his deeds than by his teachings."[26] When Gregory went to live in Neocaesarea, there were only seventeen Christians there. By the time he died forty years later, there were only seventeen non-Christians left in the city! Saint Basil writes of him:

By the co-working of the Spirit the power he had over demons was tremendous. . . . By Christ's mighty name he commanded even rivers to change their course, and caused a lake, which gave grounds for a quarrel among some greedy brethren, to dry up. His predictions of things to come in no way fell short of those of the great prophets.[27]

Saint Patrick, the apostle to Ireland, was known for extraordinary spiritual gifts. He first arrived on the island as a teenager, kidnapped from his native Britain and sold as a slave. Although he had previously been a lukewarm Christian, he prayed constantly and became fervent in his faith. He escaped Ireland when God instructed him to do so in a dream. Years later, at home in Britain, he received a vision in the night in which he saw a man called Victor who had come from Ireland with a bundle of letters. As Patrick read the opening words of one letter, he sensed many Irish voices shouting, "We ask you, boy, come and walk once more among us." He was cut to the heart, and in obedience to the vision he returned to Ireland, this time to preach the Gospel to the Irish pagans. Hundreds of healings, raisings of the dead and other miracles are attributed to Patrick. Although in this case it is difficult to separate fact from legend, it is certain that the miracles Patrick worked were a major part of the reason for the extraordinarily rapid conversion of the whole island to Christianity. Saint Augustine of Canterbury, the sixth-century apostle to the English, is likewise said to have performed many miracles.

Tongues

It is often assumed that the gift of tongues ceased after the New Testament era, since the church fathers rarely speak of it. But, in fact, the gift did continue, under a different name: *jubilation*. The church fathers used the term *tongues* for the version of this gift that was manifested at Pentecost, when the crowd miraculously heard the apostles speaking in their native languages (see Acts 2:4–11). On the other hand, jubilation referred to the version of this gift that Paul describes in 1 Corinthians 12–14: joyful praise of God that overflows aloud in an unintelligible language. Saint Augustine describes jubilation this way:

> One who jubilates does not utter words, but a certain sound of joy without words: for it is the voice of the soul poured forth in joy, expressing, as far as possible, what it feels without reflecting on the meaning. Rejoicing in exultation, one uses words that cannot be spoken and understood, but he simply lets his joy burst forth without words; his voice then appears to express a happiness so intense that he cannot explain it.[28]

Augustine encourages his congregation to jubilate and not to refrain from praising God just because they cannot find the right words: "Rejoice and speak. If you cannot express your joy, jubilate: jubilation expresses your joy if you cannot speak. Let not your joy be silent."[29] Saint Gregory the Great (Pope Saint Gregory I) adds that such praise can also be expressed in bodily gestures: "What we call jubilation is an unspeakable joy which can neither be concealed nor expressed in words. It shows itself, however, by certain gestures.[30]

During the ancient liturgy, the congregation would often jubilate together and sing spontaneous melodies under the inspiration of the Holy Spirit. Saint John Chrysostom writes, "Though men and women, young and old, are different, when they sing hymns, their voices are influenced by the Holy Spirit in such a way that the melody sounds as if sung by one voice."[31]

The fifth-century monk Saint John Cassian reports that sometimes a monk would be so filled with "inexpressible delight and keenness of spirit" that he would actually break forth into shouts of incontrollable joy that could be heard in the cells of neighboring monks. At other times the Holy Spirit would bring a profound quiet, so that "the overawed spirit either keeps all its feelings to itself or loses them and pours forth its desires to God with groanings that cannot be uttered."[32]

The decline of the gifts

In the centuries following the Patristic era, the use of spiritual gifts waned, although they never completely disappeared from the life of the Church. There were several reasons for this decline. First, the legalization of Christianity in the fourth century meant that it was now safe and sometimes even socially advantageous to become a Christian. This new situation led to a large influx of new converts, not all with the same sincerity or fervor as earlier generations. Consequently, there was a lowering of standards for baptismal preparation. It was no longer common to expect supernatural gifts as a normal effect of receiving the Holy Spirit at baptism. In addition, more Christians were being baptized as infants, with the risk that as they grew to adulthood, not all would personally appropriate the new life they had received or develop a living faith in Christ.

Second, the Montanist movement, which put an exaggerated emphasis on prophecy, led to a reaction against all charismatic manifestations. The Montanists made strange prophetic declarations and saw themselves as having a higher authority than the bishops. As a result, the movement came to be regarded as heretical, and many church leaders became wary of charisms in general.

Third, some Christians were influenced by strains of thought that tended to denigrate the body. Instead of seeing the human body as fundamentally good because God created it, as Scripture teaches, they viewed it as a kind of prison that weighs down the soul. This body-soul dualism led many Christians to deemphasize physical healings and to overemphasize asceticism and severe mortification of the body.

Finally, there was a growing tendency to identify supernatural charisms with special holiness, beyond what ordinary Christians were capable of. Gifts that had been widely experienced in the early centuries gradually came to be associated only with monks and nuns who practiced strict asceticism. As a result, it came to be considered a sign of presumption and pride for laypeople to seek supernatural gifts.

For all these reasons, the charisms were less in evidence in later centuries, although healings, miracles, prophecies and other supernatural manifestations did continue to occur. Among Catholic saints, Francis of Assisi (thirteenth century) worked many miracles, including the healing of a crippled woman and a man who had seizures, and the taming of a wolf that had terrorized a village. Gertrude the Great (thirteenth century) received supernatural visions and revelations. Catherine of Siena (fourteenth century) healed many sick people, reconciled bitter enemies and raised her own mother from the dead. Vincent Ferrer (fourteenth century) had the gift of speaking in languages he had never learned and was said to have raised more than thirty people from the dead. Francis Xavier (sixteenth century) saved the crew of a ship on which he was sailing. They had been without fresh water for three weeks and he blessed some seawater, which then became drinkable. Teresa of Avila (sixteenth century) raised up her nephew, who had been crushed by a collapsing wall. John Bosco (nineteenth century) had an extraordinary gift of prophecy. John Vianney (nineteenth century) and Pio of Pietrelcina (twentieth century) were known for the gift of reading people's hearts (see 1 Corinthians 14:24–25). Blessed Solanus Casey (twentieth century) healed countless sick people who came to him for prayer.

Many Protestants also had healing ministries prior to the twentieth century. In the seventeenth century, George Fox, founder of the Religious Society of Friends (Quakers), had over 150 recorded healings. The eighteenth-century Brethren movement believed in healing. The nineteenth century was filled with healings. The German Lutheran Johann Blumhardt experienced healings and deliverances, as did Switzerland's Dorothea Trudel, Samuel Zeller and Otto Stockmayer. Key leaders in this area from North America included Ethan O. Allen, Elizabeth Mix, Charles Cullis, William Broadman, A. J. Gordon, R. L. Stanton, A. B. Simpson and Carrie Judd Montgomery. In fact, prior to the twentieth century there was an explosion of Protestants with healing ministries; other key names included England's Charles H. Spurgeon and South Africa's Andrew Murray.[33]

These are just a few of the supernatural manifestations that continued throughout the centuries of Church history, yet such healings and miracles were no longer common in the lives of ordinary Christians on anything like the scale they had been in the early Church. That is, until recently. . . . In the next chapter, we will look at the extraordinary resurgence of the Pentecostal fire of the Holy Spirit that has taken place in the last century. But first, let's take a look at the inner experience of God's power.

The Sober Intoxication of the Spirit

When the Holy Spirit comes powerfully into a person's life, the manifestation of charisms is not the only result. Often, there is also an experience of being so overwhelmed by God's power and love that the person starts to feel, and act, inebriated—they are "beside themselves" (see 2 Corinthians 5:13). This is what happened on the Day of Pentecost, when some skeptical bystanders saw the behavior of the disciples and came up with the only explanation they could think of: "They are filled with new wine" (Acts 2:13). Ironically, there was truth in that disdainful comment. In the prophets, "new wine" was an image of the abundance of divine life that God would pour out when the Messiah came: "'Behold, the days are coming,' declares the LORD, 'when . . . the mountains shall drip sweet wine, and all the hills shall flow with it'" (Amos 9:13). At Pentecost, that "new wine" of the Spirit came!

The fathers of the Church were well aware of this irony, and they enjoyed commenting on it. Saint Ambrose of Milan writes in one of his hymns, "Let us drink with joy the sober intoxication of the Spirit!"[34] Saint Cyril of Jerusalem explains to catechumens preparing for baptism,

> They [the disciples at Pentecost] are not drunk in the way you might think. They are indeed drunk, but with the sober intoxication that kills sin and gives life to the heart and which is the opposite of physical drunkenness. Drunkenness makes a person forget what he knows; this kind, instead, brings

understanding of things that were not formerly known. They are drunk insofar as they have drunk the wine of that mystical vine which affirms, "I am the vine, you are the branches" (John 15:5).[35]

Saint Augustine adds,

> The Holy Spirit . . . found you thirsty and He has intoxicated you. May He truly intoxicate you! The Apostle said, "Do not be drunk with wine which leads to debauchery." Then, as if to clarify what we *should* be intoxicated with, he adds, "But be filled with the Spirit, addressing one another in psalms and hymns and spiritual songs, singing and making melody to the Lord with all your heart" (Eph 5:18–19). Doesn't a person who rejoices in the Lord and sings to Him exuberantly seem like a person who is drunk? I like this kind of intoxication. The Spirit of God is both drink and light.[36]

For most of Church history, it was taken for granted that receiving the Holy Spirit was *a fact of experience*, as it was for the early Christians in Acts—not something you merely accepted by faith. Augustine said in one of his sermons,

> Thanks be to the Lord our God, and wave upon wave of praise to that God to whom praise songs are due in Zion. Thanks be to him to whom we have been singing with devoted hearts and mouths, God, who is like you?, because we can feel the holy love of him deeply ensconced in your hearts, because you revere him as Lord, love him as Father. Thanks be to him who is desired before he is seen and whose presence is felt. . . .[37]

The thirteenth century's Saint Thomas Aquinas is rightly thought of as a man of the intellect, a master of logical thought and careful distinctions. But few realize that Thomas was also a man inebriated with the love of God. The same Thomas who wrote the *Summa Theologica* also wrote this:

> Spiritual refreshment consists of two things: the gifts of God and his sweetness. With reference to the first, [Scripture] says: "they shall be drunk with the abundance of your house" [Ps 36:9]. The house is the Church [1 Tim 3:15]. . . . "They shall be drunk" insofar as desires are fulfilled beyond all measure of merit, for drunkenness is a kind of excess. . . . People who are drunk are not inside but outside themselves. Thus those filled with spiritual gifts have all their attention on God. And they are refreshed not only by these gifts but also by love of God. . . . And you shall make them drink of the torrent of your pleasure. This is the love of the Holy Spirit that causes a force in the soul like a torrent. And it is a torrent of pleasure because it causes pleasure and sweetness in the soul.[38]

Blessed John Ruusbroec, a Dutch mystic of the fourteenth century, wrote of the startling effects of such spiritual inebriation:

> Spiritual inebriation means that a person receives more perceptible savor and delight than his heart or desire could long for or contain. Spiritual inebriation produces much strange behavior in a person. It makes one person sing and praise God out of the fullness of his joy, and it makes another shed many tears because of the delight he feels within his heart. In one it produces restlessness in all his limbs, causing him to run and jump and dance about, and in another the force of this inebriation is so great that he must clap his hands in jubilation. One person cries out in a loud voice and so makes manifest the fullness which he feels within, and

another becomes silent and seems to melt away out of the delight he feels in all his senses. . . . At times this delight becomes so intense that it seems to such a person that his heart will break because of all these manifold gifts and wonderful works.[39]

Just as in the age of the apostles, the sober intoxication of the Spirit is often experienced as a communal phenomenon rather than just an individual experience. In the Middle Ages, as Franciscan and Dominican friars went from town to town preaching, there were revivals that included processions with banners, torches and jubilant praise of God. A thirteenth-century Franciscan chronicler gives an account of these revivals:

> It was a time of merriment and gladness, of joy and exultation, of praise and jubilation. During this time men of all sorts sang songs of praise to God. . . . Old people and young people were of one mind. This turning to God was experienced in all the cities of Italy, and they came from the villages to the town with banners, a great multitude of people, men and women, boys and girls together, to hear the preaching and to praise God. The songs that they sang were of God, not of man, and all walked in the way of salvation. . . . Sermons were preached in the evening, in the morning and at noon. . . . Men took their places in churches and outdoors and lifted up their hands to God, to praise and bless him forever and ever. They [wished] they would never have to stop praising God, they were so drunk with his love.[40]

Revivals in our own time (Randy)

While I was attending seminary, Dr. Lewis Drummond told me about the great Shantung revival among the North

China Mission of the Southern Baptist Convention in 1932. I had never read anything about this revival until I read the book *The Shantung Revival*, which I later reprinted.[41] In the spring of 1994, I felt for several weeks recurring impulses to locate and read everything written about the Shantung revival. I was captivated by this revival, which occurred among Southern Baptist missionaries. The story made it clear that it began among the leadership, who were tired and burned out. They admitted their need for more and discovered that some of the leaders among them were not even truly born again. The emphasis of this revival was the study of the Bible, particularly relating to the Holy Spirit and a baptism of the Holy Spirit, and making sure one had been truly born again. As I read *The Shantung Revival*, I found everything that had been happening in the Toronto Blessing and other revivals throughout history—the shaking, the falling, the crying, the laughing, the sensing of electricity in the body and the healings. In fact, these things seem to happen everywhere people have been seeking the fullness of the Holy Spirit and are desperate for God and His empowerment unto salvation.

The Toronto Blessing, which began in January 1994, was the longest protracted revival meeting in the history of North America. It began when I went to the Toronto Vineyard church to preach for only four nights. The Holy Spirit fell in power, which led to nightly meetings that continued for more than twelve years and were attended by millions of visitors from around the world. Since then, the revival has impacted thousands of churches and millions of believers. As a result of lives touched in the Toronto Blessing, well over twenty thousand churches have been started in various parts of the world, leading to more than four million new converts to Christ.

Later in 1994, I met an evangelist in Toronto who had previously evangelized an indigenous people group in the Russian Far East. He had left the people with copies of the New Testament in their language. When he returned there a short time after the Toronto revival had broken out, there were episodes of the congregants appearing drunk in the Spirit. He asked them who had come to them from Toronto, and the congregants told him they had never heard of Toronto. They explained that they had read Acts chapter 2. What happened to these congregants in Russia had begun in January 1994, the same month that the Toronto outpouring began.

On another occasion, I met apostolic missionary David Hogan from Mexico. In the mountains of southern Mexico, he oversaw Native Americans who were illiterate and lived without electricity or radios. Cultural norms prohibited them from showing emotion—no joy at weddings, no sorrow at funerals. Yet on one visit, he found them laughing and behaving as if drunk, under the power of the Spirit. David was aware of what was happening in Toronto, and he realized that God was pouring out His Spirit there in Mexico, on these isolated, illiterate people who had no way of knowing what God was doing in other parts of the world. This occurrence in southern Mexico also took place in the first few months of 1994, at the start of the Toronto outpouring.

Later, I heard the testimony of Dennis Balcomb, a missionary and apostolic leader in China. He told me that the same phenomena—believers appearing as if drunk—occurred in January 1994 in what had been the Shantung Province of China. This people group, like the Indians of southern

Mexico and the indigenous group in Russia, had no knowledge or awareness of what God was doing in Toronto. All of these experiences were sovereign visitations of the Holy Spirit, as happened at the first Pentecost.

We have taken a look at how the gifts of the Spirit were operating in the age of the apostles and the age of the church fathers. We have heard from great men of the faith such as Cyril of Jerusalem, Augustine, Thomas Aquinas and others who knew what it was to be soberly intoxicated with God's power and love. In the next chapter we bring our focus closer to the present day, as we turn our attention to the extraordinary resurgence of the Pentecostal fire of the Holy Spirit in the last century—fire on the earth!

4

Fire on the Earth

s Jesus was journeying toward Jerusalem, where He knew that arrest, torture and death awaited Him, He cried out, "I came to cast fire on the earth, and would that it were already kindled!" (Luke 12:49). Even though His Passion would mean unspeakable agony, Jesus longed to go through with it because of the stupendous result it would bring about: the fire of God being cast upon the earth. Jesus' longing for that fire on the earth was fulfilled fifty days after His resurrection, on the Day of Pentecost, when the Holy Spirit fell on His disciples in the Upper Room, with the appearance of tongues as of fire (see Acts 2:1–4). The Holy Spirit caused the disciples to be set ablaze with God's love and be conduits for that love to flow freely to others.

Jesus again foretold that same outpouring of the Holy Spirit just before He ascended into heaven: "John baptized with water, but you will be baptized with the Holy Spirit. . . . You will receive power when the Holy Spirit has come upon you" (Acts 1:5, 8). The fire of God would be at the same time a waterfall from heaven that would *baptize* (immerse, plunge, drench) the believers in the very life of God. Jesus' prophecy was fulfilled on the Day of Pentecost. As Paul puts it, "God's love has been poured into our hearts through the Holy Spirit who has been given to us" (Romans 5:5). But Pentecost was never meant to be a once-and-gone blessing. Throughout the book of Acts, it is clear that the apostles sought to ensure that each group of newly baptized converts received the same gift they had received: to be immersed, flooded and inundated with divine life in a way that was outwardly evident.[1]

The term "baptism in the Holy Spirit" is used by Christians around the world today—Catholics, Protestants and Orthodox believers—to refer to an experience of the Holy Spirit breaking into their life in a new and powerful way, as happened to the early Christians on the Day of Pentecost. Although different Christians would define it differently, the baptism in the Holy Spirit can be described as an outpouring of the Holy Spirit into one's life, bringing a profound revelation of the love of God the Father, the lordship of Jesus and the power of the Spirit and His gifts (see Acts 1:8; Romans 5:5; Ephesians 1:16–22). It is this immersion in the Holy Spirit that causes the spiritual gifts to spring forth in a person's life and to be activated for the spread of the Gospel.

The Twentieth-Century Outpouring

Over the last century, hundreds of millions of Christians have experienced the baptism in the Spirit in a way that has radically transformed their lives. The fact that God began to pour out His Spirit in such a dramatic way in modern times was a surprise. Rare was the church or denomination looking for this kind of renewal. No human being planned it. But in retrospect, it is possible to see the hand of God at work behind the events of history, even across historic lines of division among Christians, preparing His people for this new tsunami of the Spirit.

In the Catholic Church of the nineteenth century, the Holy Spirit had become what some theologians have termed "the forgotten Person of the Trinity." Many traditional works of spirituality hardly mentioned the very source of spirituality, the Holy Spirit. There were some formal prayers to the Holy Spirit, but little expectation that He would actually come in a perceptible way.

But God was at work behind the scenes. In the late 1800s an Italian Catholic religious sister named Elena Guerra (now honored in the Catholic Church as Blessed Elena Guerra) sensed that God was leading her to spread devotion to the Holy Spirit. She founded a religious order devoted to the Holy Spirit and formed prayer groups that she called "Pentecost Upper Rooms." Her hope was that the Church would be united in constant prayer for the coming of the Spirit, and that "Come, Holy Spirit" would be a prayer on the lips of every Catholic.

Sister Elena felt called by God to write a series of confidential letters to the Pope, at that time Leo XIII, telling him that God desired to renew the Church through a return to the Holy Spirit. Amazingly enough, Pope Leo paid attention to her appeals. In response, he wrote a letter to all the Catholic bishops of the world, asking the whole church to pray a novena to the Holy Spirit every year, leading up to the feast of Pentecost.[2] A novena is nine days of prayer, based on the original "novena," the disciples' prayer in the Upper Room, between Jesus' ascension and Pentecost (see Acts 1:14).[3] Curiously, the specific intention that Pope Leo asked Catholics to pray for during this novena was Christian unity—and this was at a time when "ecumenism" was not in the vocabulary of either Catholics or Protestants, and each side viewed the other as simply condemned!

Unfortunately, many bishops ignored Pope Leo's request. Sister Elena told the Pope she was pleased with his efforts but disappointed with the poor response of bishops. She then begged the Pope to dedicate the new century that was about to begin to the Holy Spirit. So he did: On January 1, 1901, Pope Leo opened the century by praying the ancient hymn "Come Creator Spirit" (*Veni Creator Spiritus*), invoking the Holy Spirit upon the new century on behalf of the whole Church.

Unbeknownst to Pope Leo, *on that very same day*, halfway around the world, in Topeka, Kansas, the Holy Spirit fell upon a little Protestant group, the Bethel Bible School, with the manifestation of tongues and other charismatic gifts. This outpouring later spread to Azusa Street, Los Angeles, marking the beginning of the twentieth-century Pentecostal revival. Around the same time, there were similar outpourings of the Spirit in the Welsh Revival of 1904; at a girls' school in Mukti, India, in 1905; at a Methodist church in Santiago, Chile, in 1905; in Pyongyang, Korea, in 1907; and in Belem, Brazil, in 1911. From all of these places, missionaries went out all over the world to evangelize and the Pentecostal revival spread like wildfire, to the point that it has now reached more than 700 million people around the world.

But God was not finished yet.

The Duquesne Weekend

At first, most of those whom the Pentecostal revival touched were not accepted by their churches, so they formed new denominations. But in the 1950s and '60s the revival began to come into the historic Protestant denominations. Episcopalians, Lutherans, Methodists and Baptists who were baptized in the Spirit remained within their churches and began to renew them from within.

Meanwhile, God was preparing the way in the Catholic Church, especially through Vatican Council II (1961–1965). Pope John XXIII asked all Catholics to pray daily during the years of the council, *Lord, renew Your wonders in this our day, as by a new Pentecost!* At the council, the bishops for the first time in centuries officially affirmed that the Holy Spirit's charisms are necessary to the life of the Church. Pope John Paul II later expressed the significance of this breakthrough:

> Whenever the Spirit intervenes, he leaves people astonished. He brings about events of amazing newness; he radically changes persons and history. This was the unforgettable experience of the Second Vatican Council during which . . . the Church rediscovered the charismatic dimension as one of her constitutive elements.[4]

The council strongly affirmed the ongoing role of the gifts of the Spirit and called bishops and priests to welcome them gratefully, while also discerning their right use:

> It is not only through the sacraments and the ministries of the Church that the Holy Spirit sanctifies and leads the people of God . . . , but, "allotting his gifts to everyone according as He wills" (1 Cor 12:11), He distributes special graces among

the faithful of every rank. . . . These charisms, whether they are the more outstanding or the more simple and widely diffused, are to be received with thanksgiving and consolation for they are perfectly suited to and useful for the needs of the Church.[5]

It was not accidental that only two years after Vatican Council II, in 1967, the outpouring of the Spirit that had spread among Protestants came into the Catholic Church. It began at a retreat held for a group of college students from Duquesne University in Pittsburgh.[6] The two faculty moderators of this group had been experiencing a hunger for more of the Holy Spirit. A few weeks before the retreat, they decided to seek out charismatic Christians—a very unusual step for Catholics at that time. They heard about an interdenominational charismatic prayer group nearby, and they decided to go. God had prepared the leader of this group, a housewife named Flo Dodge. She sensed the significance of Catholics coming to receive the Holy Spirit, and she felt led to allow no one in her prayer group to lay hands on the two Catholics, so that no one could take credit for the baptism in the Holy Spirit coming into the Catholic Church. The group prayed for the two faculty members, and they were baptized in the Holy Spirit.

The faculty moderators did not tell the students what had happened to them at the prayer group, but in preparation for the retreat, which would take place a few weeks later, they asked them to read chapters 1–4 of Acts, and also a book by Pentecostal preacher David Wilkerson, *The Cross and the Switchblade*.

On the retreat weekend, the students sang the same ancient hymn Pope Leo had sung to open the century, *Veni*

Creator Spiritus. They prayed for God to deepen the grace of their confirmation. At one point the plumbing at the retreat center broke down, and the students were told they might have to go home. So they prayed fervently for God to send water . . . and He answered their prayer in more ways than one! The plumbing was fixed, and when one student, David Mangan, went into the little Eucharistic chapel to thank God, he was immediately overwhelmed by the presence of God. He found himself flat on his face, prostrate before the Lord, completely immersed in God's love, praising Him in an unknown language. One by one, other students came into the chapel and in a similar way were flooded with the glory of God. Almost immediately, they began to praise God in tongues—some without knowing what this gift was—and to manifest other gifts of the Spirit.

One of the participants on that retreat eloquently summed up what had happened:

> Our faith has come alive, our believing has become a kind of knowing. Suddenly, the world of the supernatural has become more real than the natural. . . . Jesus Christ is a real person to us, a real person who is Our Lord and who is active in our lives. We read the New Testament as though it were literally true, now, every word, every line. Prayer and the sacraments have become truly our daily bread instead of practices which we recognize as "good for us." A love of Scripture, a love of the Church I never thought possible, a transformation of our relationships with others, a need and a power of witness beyond all expectation, have all become part of our lives. . . . We have also been showered with charismata.[7]

The outpouring that began at Duquesne spread with re-markable rapidity to Catholics on other college campuses, and then throughout the world. Today, an estimated 150 million Catholics have experienced the baptism in the Holy Spirit.[8] For many, it has awakened them from spiritual complacency into a life of passionate love of Christ. For others, it has catapulted them into mission, including evangelization, healing and deliverance ministries, service to the poor and lay leadership in the Catholic Church.

From the beginning of this twentieth-century outpouring, both Protestants and Catholics have sought to understand theologically what God has done. How does the baptism in the Holy Spirit relate to initial conversion to Christ? How does it relate to the sacraments of baptism and confirmation? For Catholics, this is an especially important question since the Catholic Church teaches that we receive the Holy Spirit in baptism, and again in a fuller way at confirmation. Is it possible to receive more of the Spirit?

In the rest of this chapter, we will briefly describe the differing answers that have been given to these questions. We will then explain how a person can receive baptism in the Spirit.

Different Perspectives on the Baptism

Among Protestants, there are four main perspectives regarding the baptism in the Holy Spirit. These positions are:

1. Baptism in the Spirit is an activation, or a coming alive, of what was given through faith at the time of regeneration (the new birth in Christ). This is the view of most historical evangelical denominations.

2. Baptism in the Spirit is an experience of the Spirit that is subsequent to receiving the Spirit in regeneration.

The Holiness and Pentecostal denominations hold this perspective.

3. Baptism in the Spirit is not connected to regeneration in Christ, but is a new coming of the Spirit into a person's life for a new mission or calling.

4. Baptism in the Spirit is a historically significant global phenomenon that signals an eschatological turning point.

Among Catholics, there are variations of each of these four positions, with the majority holding a version of the first view, that it is an activation, or a coming alive, of what was already given at the time of sacramental baptism.[9]

Baptism in the Spirit as an activation

This view of baptism in the Spirit—as an activation, or a coming alive, of what was already given through faith and baptism—understands baptism in the Spirit to occur at the moment of regeneration (or, for Catholics, in the sacrament of baptism). It recognizes, however, that most people do not experience this reality at the time, either because they were baptized as infants or because they were not in an environment of expectant faith. It is not that nothing occurred, but rather the gift of the Spirit is dormant in the person's life. Later, often in the context of receiving prayer to be filled with the Holy Spirit, this gift is activated. This later experience is not a receiving of the Spirit, but a stirring up or a release of the Holy Spirit, who was already present in the individual.

Randy: The American Baptist Dr. Clayton Ford, who for many years was the leader of the Charismatic Fellowship of the American Baptist denomination, held this view.[10] Dr. Ford asked me to speak a few years back at their annual meeting. While there, I heard him use this illustration to explain the baptism in the Spirit. Think of Christmas as a symbol for our new birth or regeneration in Christ. Eternal life is given at this time, represented by a large bag left by Santa Claus. Many people rush down to the tree when they awaken and open the bag and take out a gift, i.e., salvation. From that moment, all the gifts in the bag belong to them. After unwrapping the gift of salvation, however, they stop looking in the bag. Later, someone tells them there are more gifts in that bag. It may be a short time since opening the first gift or a much longer time. When they realize they have not opened all their gifts, they return to the bag and find the other gifts. These are not new gifts given later. They have been theirs all along, but they had not opened them. They had not appropriated what was already theirs.[11]

Gordon Fee, a New Testament scholar and a classical Pentecostal in the Assemblies of God, believes Scripture teaches that baptism in the Spirit with His gifts is usually simultaneous with conversion.[12] But because of a lack of proper preaching and understanding about the Holy Spirit, for most people today there is a disconnect, resulting in their experience of the baptism coming after conversion. This is not because it is the New Testament pattern, but because at this time in the history of the Church, there is not faith to receive all at once. Many Christians today are like the disciples of John the Baptist whom Paul met in Ephesus. They said, "We have not even heard that there is a Holy Spirit" (Acts 19:2).

Among Catholics, this view of baptism in the Spirit—as an actualizing or a bringing alive of what was already given at baptism—is the most common view. It was the position held by Cardinal Léon Joseph Suenens, who was one of the leading bishops at Vatican Council II. It is also held by Dr. Ralph Martin, and by Father Raniero Cantalamessa, Preacher to the Papal Household, among others.[13] These theologians note that some of the church fathers used the term "baptism in the Spirit" to refer to the sacraments of baptism and confirmation—usually administered together to adult converts—because the new Christians experienced what the New Testament describes as the normal effects of receiving the Holy Spirit: life-changing knowledge of the Father's love, joy in living under the lordship of Jesus, over-flowing praise of God, a zeal to bear witness to Christ and the manifestation of the gifts of the Spirit. As Christianity developed and infant baptism became the norm, however, it became increasingly possible to receive the sacraments without their intended effects.[14] In such a case, the person truly receives the Holy Spirit, but the gift remains unopened.[15] It is like having a deed to a vast tract of land—a kingdom—bequeathed to you as an inheritance, yet this deed remains a document locked away in a filing cabinet in the attorney's office. Many Christians are not living in the Kingdom they have inherited. Their lives are not showing forth what are meant to be the normal effects of these sacraments. In such cases, there is need for a fresh outpouring of the Holy Spirit in order to experience the fullness of what God has for us. So today, "baptism in the Spirit" usually refers to that later experience, when the gift already received is "fanned into flame" (2 Timothy 1:6).

Another analogy both Catholics and Protestants often use to explain this position is that our lives are like a glass of milk. When we first came to faith in Christ, or when we were baptized in water (sacramental baptism), we were reborn in Christ. At that moment chocolate syrup, representing the Holy Spirit, was poured into our glass. He has been there ever since, but for many, the chocolate syrup simply sits in the bottom of the glass, needing to be stirred up to color and flavor the milk in a much greater way. Baptism in the Spirit is the stirring up of the chocolate.

Baptism in the Spirit as subsequent to regeneration

A second view is that baptism in the Spirit is distinct from and subsequent to the new birth in Christ. This view entered Protestantism through the Anglican priest John Wesley (1703–1791), who became the founder of the Methodist denomination, the spiritual father of the Wesleyan Holiness denominations, and the grandfather of the Pentecostal denominations.

Wesley was concerned about the overemphasis on imputed righteousness without enough emphasis on experiential righteousness. He thought the spiritual state of many people in the Protestant churches in England was deplorably inadequate. They were living with little victory over sin in their lives. He believed it was possible to have a subsequent experience with the Holy Spirit that gave Christians power to have much greater victory over sin. The goal was not only to experience salvation, but also to become more Christlike in character. The Christian life was more than being justified; it was to include sanctification, which would come in a work of the Spirit subsequent to regeneration. Although various terms were used for this experience, during the last twenty years of Wesley's life it was most often called the baptism in the Spirit.

Wesley, being Anglican, had a deep appreciation for the writings of the fathers of the Church. Anglicanism was the Protestant national church of England, a nation that had previously been Catholic. Wesley was not as heavily influenced as earlier Protestants by the teachings of the Protestant Reformation, especially the Reformed emphasis on receiving regeneration and sanctification at the same time. From the writings of the church fathers, he knew that in the early Church people were regenerated by a work of the Spirit in water baptism, and immediately following baptism were filled with the Spirit when they received the laying on of hands or anointing with sacred oil. Later, in the Latin Rite of the Catholic Church, there was a separation between these two events, regeneration by the Spirit in baptism and a fuller giving of the Spirit in confirmation.[16] People were usually baptized as infants and confirmed some years later. Wesley was influenced by this understanding of a fuller giving of the Spirit years after baptism.

Among Catholics, theologian Stephen B. Clark, one of the earliest participants in the Catholic Charismatic Renewal, holds a variation of this view.[17] Clark holds that baptism in the Holy Spirit is a release of the power of the Spirit given in confirmation. He links baptism in the Spirit to confirmation rather than to baptism, because of its "Pentecostal" nature, as seen in Acts and in Catholic teaching. Confirmation is not just a deepening of one's relationship with Christ, but a new outpouring of the Spirit and His gifts, equipping a person to share in the mission of the Church. In fact, the

Catholic Church teaches that "the effect of the sacrament of Confirmation is the special outpouring of the Holy Spirit as once granted to the apostles on the day of Pentecost."[18] The Church regards the origin of confirmation as the event recorded in Acts 8, when the apostles laid hands on the new believers in Samaria who had already been baptized, and the Holy Spirit "fell upon them" in a dramatic and perceptible way (see Acts 8:14–18). Thus, confirmation in its very essence is linked to the "Pentecostal" outpouring of the Holy Spirit and His gifts. Yet few of those who are confirmed today manifest anything like what Scripture and the Church hold as the intended effects of that sacrament. On the other hand, when people experience baptism in the Holy Spirit, sometimes years later, their lives do begin to manifest the normal effects of confirmation.

Among those who see baptism in the Spirit as subsequent to conversion, some (mostly Pentecostals) consider the gift of tongues as the necessary initial evidence that a person has been baptized in the Spirit. Others (mostly evangelicals and Catholics) believe instead that tongues can be *evidence*, but not *the only initial evidence* that someone has been baptized in the Spirit.

Baptism in the Spirit as a new sending

A third perspective views baptism in the Spirit as a new sending of the Spirit for a new mission or calling. It is a fact of past and present experience that the Holy Spirit sometimes comes into a person's life in a new way for a new mission or calling. This view also has biblical support. For example, Jesus had been conceived by the Holy Spirit and was already full of the Spirit (see John 3:34; Colossians 2:9), yet the Holy

Spirit came upon Him in a new way at His baptism. His baptism marked the beginning of His ministry, and it was connected to the purpose of His mission. "Now when all the people were baptized, and when Jesus also had been baptized and was praying, the heavens were opened, and the Holy Spirit descended on him. . . . Jesus, when he *began his ministry*, was about thirty years of age" (Luke 3:21–23, emphasis added).

Jesus' first sermon in Nazareth again connects the anointing of the Spirit to His mission: "The Spirit of the Lord is upon me, because he has anointed me to proclaim good news to the poor . . ." (Luke 4:18).

Among Catholics, Father Francis Sullivan holds this understanding of baptism in the Spirit as a new sending of the Spirit into a person's life for a new mission.[19] He points out that Saint Thomas Aquinas speaks about the possibility of such a new work of the Spirit in a person:

> There is an invisible sending [of the Holy Spirit] also in respect to an advance in virtue or an increase of grace. . . . Such an invisible sending is especially to be seen in that kind of increase of grace whereby a person moves forward to some new act or new state of grace: as, for instance, when a person moves forward into the grace of working miracles, or of prophecy, or out of the burning love of God offers his life as a martyr, or renounces all of his possessions, or undertakes some other such arduous thing.[20]

This view takes into account the fact that baptism in the Spirit is truly an action of the Holy Spirit, and not merely a human work of "activating" the gift of the Spirit through deeper faith and commitment to Christ. It involves not only what is already given, but also a new impartation of power from above.

Mary: Someone I know who received baptism in the Spirit this way is Sister Miriam Duggan from Ireland. She was already totally devoted to Christ as a Franciscan missionary and obstetrician, ministering to the poorest of the poor in Uganda. But when she experienced baptism in the Spirit, her ministry went to a whole new level. She began to pray for her patients as the Holy Spirit led, and began to see healings and miracles. Then she was led to found a youth chastity program that contributed to reducing the AIDS epidemic throughout the entire continent of Africa.

Randy: I know ministers who were already baptized in the Holy Spirit, but who had another baptism in the Holy Spirit, the purpose of which seems to have been to catapult them into a new mission or to cause their present mission or ministry to explode to a much higher level of effectiveness. Three people who illustrate this truth are Dr. Leif Hetland, Dr. Heidi Baker and Rev. Marcelo Casagrande.

Dr. Leif Hetland is an international evangelist and missiologist. As I mentioned in chapter 1, he has led over one million to the Lord all over the world through his "Healing Celebrations." Years ago, Leif was a Baptist pastor in Norway. He had received the gift of tongues but had not experienced any other of the gifts of the Spirit. When I prayed for him and gave him a prophecy, he fell to the ground, began to tremble and shake from the power of God coursing through his body, and could not get off the floor for almost three hours. The following week, he experienced words of knowledge, prophetic gifts, and gifts of healing and miracles for the first time.

The prophecy was, "I see you in a dark place. All around you is darkness, but God will make you light in the darkness. You're going to make a way where there is no way. God is going to make you a bulldozer. I see a multitude of people following you out of the darkness into the light." Immediately following this prophecy, Leif experienced the baptism in the Spirit that activated and empowered him in a new way.

Leif did not understand how to interpret the prophecy or how to apply it. But about a year later, he did his first ministry in a non-Christian country in the Middle East. This is where he has seen so much fruit, so many healings and so many of another religion profess faith in Jesus after they see the miracles and healings done in His name. Before the new baptism in the Spirit there were no healings, miracles, words of knowledge or prophecies associated with Leif's life, and he had not led hundreds of thousands, let alone over a million, to Christ.

Heidi Baker's experience was rather close in time to Leif's. Heidi had her fresh baptism in Toronto, at the church where the outpouring occurred that became known as the Toronto Blessing. I was preaching on pressing in for a greater touch from God when Heidi came forward. At the time, she was not well-known. I had never met her. The pastor of the church, John Arnott, had pointed her out to me, told me her name and told me she was a missionary in Mozambique. He also told me that she was spiritually exhausted. She had come a month earlier and had been physically healed. She had returned in hope of being spiritually renewed.

During the sermon, Heidi came to the platform and knelt in front of it, praying to God. When I saw her, I said to her,

"Heidi, God wants to know: Do you want the nation of Mozambique?"

She responded, with her eyes full of tears and her hand extended toward me, "Yesssss!"

I responded, "God is going to give you the nation of Mozambique. You are going to see the blind see, the deaf hear, the lame walk and the dead be raised."

Instantly, the power of God came upon Heidi. She began to feel heat—"as if I had been put into an oven," she told me. Power also began to flow through her body immediately following the prophecy. It became so strong that she cried out, "God, You're going to kill me!"

God responded, *Good, I need you dead.* The voice of God came to her: *Hundreds of churches and thousands of people.*

Heidi responded, *How can that be? Rolland and I have started four churches in seventeen years, and it has almost killed us!*

God gave her a vision of the twelve men she was to invite to join her and her husband, Rolland, in their work in Mozambique. Heidi's experience of power lasted seven days and nights and included electricity and heat, which caused trembling and sweating; love, which caused weeping; joy, which caused laughter; and peace, which caused a sweet resting in His presence.

This would not be the last time God would touch Heidi with such power. She would have several more fresh baptisms in the Spirit over the next years. Once in Beira, Mozambique, I was ministering when the Spirit fell upon Heidi, Rolland and all the key leaders who were present. They fell to the ground and were under the anointing of God's presence—joy, power and glory. During this experience, Heidi had a vision of ships bringing supplies to their mission among the people. She heard the voice of the Lord say, *Thousands of churches and millions of people.*

She told me this was easier to believe than the earlier word about hundreds of churches and thousands of people. That word sounded impossible at the time, but in just a few short years God had already fulfilled it with several hundred churches started and thousands of new believers in their ministry. The fulfillment of that impossible word made it possible to believe that this new word would become a reality.

God has done what He told Heidi He would do. Today they have over ten thousand churches in Mozambique and over a million followers of Jesus in those churches. The blind have seen, the deaf have heard, the lame have walked, and there are many testimonies of people being raised from the dead through the local "Partners in Harvest: Iris" pastors in Mozambique.

Marcelo Casagrande was a pastor of a Baptist church that averaged six hundred in attendance when we first met. He and some of his leaders came to a meeting where I was teaching on healing and impartation. They had to carry him out of the meeting the first and second nights because of the power on his body. He was unable to drive, and the second night he was carried into his home and was laid on the bed. He was so touched by God's power that he wept for three days and nights. He did not eat or drink for those three days. He received a mighty baptism of love and power. After this event, he began to see healings regularly, something very different from his ministry prior to this event.

Some time later, Marcelo was at another of my meetings. This time when I began to pray for him, I noticed that his hands were full of a liquid. I asked him, "Do your hands sweat more than normal?"

He answered, "No."

I instantly said to the congregation in a louder voice over the mic, "Hey, everybody! This man is receiving a miracle anointing right now!"

Marcelo fell to the ground and shook. My translator and spiritual son, Ed Rocha, placed his watch on him and said, "It is time. God is going to send you to every country in Latin America."

Marcelo did not even have a passport at the time. Before the year was over, however, he had preached in every country in Latin America. He quit counting after he had five hundred blind eyes see, five hundred deaf ears hear, five hundred tumors disappear and hundreds of people in wheelchairs or using crutches and canes walk without aid.[21]

It is not that the baptism in the Spirit only occurs in people who become famous and internationally known. There are people who are not famous but are being mightily used of God. The emergence of their newfound power and anointing came immediately following their baptism in the Spirit or impartation of the Spirit, terms that I believe can be used synonymously. For example, there is a woman I will call Sharon in one of the largest churches in Europe. She is not a key leader or on staff at a church. The first time we were at her church, she received a baptism in the Spirit.

Following her baptism in the Spirit, she began to pray for people on the streets of her city. In five years, she saw eighteen hundred people healed. Not only is that a significant number; it is an even more significant percentage. When Sharon prays for people, she sees 42 percent of them healed. It is a higher percentage than almost all of the famous healing evangelists I have studied or known. Yet Sharon is unknown. I would not have known about her, had not the executive pastor of the church told me her story and introduced her to me. Though most people on earth have never heard of Sharon, I believe her name is both known in heaven and feared in hell.

Like Sharon, there are doctors who during a service have received an impartation or baptism in the Spirit for empowerment. These doctors, from Sri Lanka, Australia, England and the United States, have seen a significant increase in healings through prayer. There are civil engineers, housewives and people from all walks of life who have also been so used.

On one trip in Brazil, I was introduced to a woman who was not even a cell group leader in her cell-based church of tens of thousands of members. The senior pastor told me about her. She had received the most powerful impartation or baptism in the Spirit, with more fruit, than any other person in his church, including the several hundred pastors. When she prayed, more people were healed, fell to the floor under God's power or were filled with the Holy Spirit than when anyone else in the church prayed.[22]

Baptism in the Spirit as an eschatological turning point

A fourth perspective on the baptism in the Spirit is that the global scale of the outpouring of the Holy Spirit and His charisms in the last century is a historically significant phenomenon that signals an eschatological turning point. This view focuses not on an individual experience, but on the wider Church.

Among Catholics, Father Peter Hocken, a British priest and historian, championed this view.[23] He pointed out that in the New Testament, John the Baptist's prophecy that Jesus would "baptize with the Holy Spirit and fire" links baptism in the Spirit with the coming of the Messianic age and eschatological (end-time) judgment. The two passages in Acts that explicitly mention this prophecy being fulfilled—Acts 1:5, referring to the first outpouring of the Spirit at Pentecost, and Acts 11:16, referring to the outpouring on Gentile believers—were decisive turning points for the Church. Peter, in his Pentecost sermon, states that what God had just done was a sign of "the last days" (Acts 2:17). Likewise, baptism in the Spirit as it is occurring today is not just a personal experience of renewal or empowerment, but a way that God is preparing His whole Church for the coming of the King and the Kingdom. This does not mean that we can predict when Jesus' Second Coming will be, only that God is preparing His people for it in a significant way in our time.

Randy: When I was in my early twenties, at The Southern Baptist Theological Seminary in Louisville, Kentucky, I was also taught in my class on Acts that the baptism in the Spirit described in Acts indicated a major event in the salvation history of God's people, signifying the move from the Old Covenant to the New Covenant people of God. It was a major historical eschatological turning point. It was also an indicator of further turning points in the history of the early Church in Acts.

The Holy Spirit coming upon groups of people was a sign of social/cultural/ethnic barriers being broken through by the Holy Spirit. As the Gospel spread from Jews to Samaritans, to God-fearing Gentiles, to pagan Gentiles, there was a witness of the Spirit that all these developments were of God. The leading of the Spirit took precedence over the word of

God given in the Old Testament regarding circumcision as the way to belong to God's people. They recognized that this outpouring meant that God was accepting Gentiles into His Church. This understanding was decisive for the Church's first general council, held in Jerusalem (see Acts 15). A major question—whether Gentiles could be included in the Church, and on what basis—was settled primarily by the activity of the Spirit in baptizing people with the gift of tongues and power that was evident to all who observed it.[24]

I believe that the outpouring of the Holy Spirit among Protestants at the beginning of the twentieth century marked an eschatological event. The 1857 sermon of the famous Baptist pastor-preacher Charles Haddon Spurgeon, "The Power of the Holy Spirit," could be seen as a prophecy—one that indicates Spurgeon was expecting a new degree of Pentecostal power and gifts, especially in the light of his closing quote from Peter's sermon on the Day of Pentecost:

Another great work of the Holy Spirit, which is not accomplished, is the bringing on of the latter-day glory. In a few more years—I know not when, I know not how—the Holy Spirit will be poured out in far different style from the present. There are diversities of operations; and during the last few years it has been the case that the diversified operations have consisted of very little pouring out of the Spirit. Ministers have gone on in dull routine, continually preaching—preaching—preaching, and little good has been done. I do hope that a fresh era has dawned upon us, and that there is a better pouring out of the Spirit even now. For the hour is coming, and it may be even now, when the Holy Ghost will be poured out again in such a wonderful manner, that many will run to and from and knowledge shall be increased—the knowledge of the Lord shall cover the earth as the waters cover the surface of the great deep; when His Kingdom shall come, and His will shall be done on earth as it is in heaven. . . . My eyes flash with the thought that very likely I shall live to see the out-pouring of the Spirit; when "the sons and the daughters of God shall prophesy, and the young men shall see visions, and the old men shall dream dreams."[25]

Within Protestantism, there were precursors to the twentieth-century Pentecostal revival. The Second Great Awakening in the early 1800s gave birth to the modern Protestant missionary movement, as well as many new ministries involving social change. The Pentecostal revival likewise impacted the world by producing a great missionary expansion, with crusade evangelism through men like T. L. Osborn, Oral Roberts, Tommy Hicks, Billy Graham and many others.

The charismatic renewal that began in historic Protestant churches in 1960 and in the Catholic Church in 1967 is another global phenomenon that signals an eschatological turning point. Besides causing hundreds of millions of Christians to come alive in their faith, it is also preparing the churches to be in a better position to fulfill Jesus' prayer that we would be one, as He and the Father are one (see John 17). Through the outpouring of the Holy Spirit, many Christians have discovered a deep kinship with one another that they never knew was possible. Believers from radically different denominations have experienced the same passionate love for Jesus, the same power of the Holy Spirit, the same manifestation of tongues and other charisms. It has become clear to many that in these times, God has initiated an ecumenical movement—an ecumenism of the Spirit.

Randy: This was not an easy thing at first for traditional Pentecostals and Baptists to accept. Both groups believe Christians should not drink any alcohol. Other fundamentalists struggled with it as well. How could the Holy Spirit fall upon wine-drinking Catholics, beer-drinking Lutherans, martini-drinking Episcopalians and Scotch-drinking Presbyterians? (It should be noted that this reference is to my experience in the United States. Once in Brazil, at a multi-thousand member Presbyterian church, I made this statement and later had to apologize to the pastor and church, not realizing this Presbyterian denomination in Brazil did not allow its members to drink alcohol.)

Mary: One of the surprises of the Spirit was that the leadership of the Catholic Church so quickly accepted the Catholic Charismatic Renewal. Many Pentecostals expected that Catholics who were baptized in the Spirit would soon be rejected by their church, as had occurred with Pentecostals. Instead, only eight years after the Catholic Charismatic Renewal began, Pope Paul VI met with thousands of Catholic charismatics in Saint Peter's Basilica in Rome and spoke of the renewal as "a chance for the church."[26] Dozens of national bishops' conferences issued statements on the renewal, which were overwhelmingly positive, although they also cautioned against the misuse of spiritual gifts.[27] Popes John Paul II and Benedict XVI also embraced the renewal, expressing the hope that it would spread "the culture of Pentecost" throughout the Church.[28] Pope Francis has gone further, telling the renewal, "I expect from you that you share with all in the Church the grace of Baptism in the Holy Spirit."[29]

Both the outpouring on Protestants at the beginning of the twentieth century, immediately after the Pope called the whole Catholic Church to a novena for the coming of the Holy Spirit, and the 1967 outpouring upon Catholics, must be seen as modern-day equivalents to Peter's experience at Cornelius's house in Acts 10. "If then God gave the same gift to them as he gave to us when we believed in the Lord Jesus Christ, who was I that I could stand in God's way?" (Acts 11:17).

Are these four viewpoints mutually incompatible?

These different understandings are not competitive interpretations, each demanding the exclusion of the others. It is not that you must choose one view and reject the others. No, this is not an *either/or*, but an *all/and* possibility. Baptism in the Spirit can have one effect or purpose in one person's life and another in another person's life. It can be both a personal impartation of the Holy Spirit to individuals and, on a wider scale, a global phenomenon that signals God's ultimate purposes for His Church.

The winds of change are blowing—and long-standing walls of division are beginning to fall. Why? Because people are no longer satisfied with tidy, supposedly theologically airtight understandings of the baptism in the Holy Spirit. Desperation has risen in the hearts of people to experience the intimate presence of God, the power of God tangibly touching us and the revelation from God by the Spirit, all of which the Bible speaks of in such experiential terms. Countless Christians have entered into this Pentecostal experience on all continents and among most denominations.

Having considered multiple ways of understanding baptism in the Holy Spirit, all of which are biblical and valid, we now turn our attention to the question of how a person can receive the baptism in the Spirit.

Receiving the Baptism in the Holy Spirit

Randy: How does someone go about receiving the baptism in the Holy Spirit? There is no one method or formula for receiving this grace, since it involves a personal relationship with the living God, who always acts freely as He wills. But there are ways we can prepare for and pursue it.

The famous nineteenth-century evangelist R. A. Torrey, who was part of the Holiness movement in America and England, offered these seven steps for obtaining baptism in the Holy Spirit:[30]

1. Repent for your sins and accept Jesus as Christ and Lord.
2. Change your mind about sin, renouncing it, and find a place of honesty in your heart.
3. Humble yourself in confession of sin.
4. Choose obedience and a "total surrender to the will of God."[31]
5. Have an intense desire in your heart to be baptized in the Holy Spirit (see Luke 11:13).
6. Ask for a blessing and baptism in the Spirit (again, see Luke 11:13). Torrey believed that "what was given to the Church must be appropriated by each believer for himself."[32]
7. Have faith in order to receive the baptism (see Mark 11:24).

Imagine what the Church would look like if every believer fully embraced these seven steps!

A. W. Tozer, the well-educated Dutch Reformed pastor, mentions in his book *How to Be Filled with the Holy Spirit* something Torrey does not—that God's plan for you most certainly involves a baptism in the Spirit. Tozer states that the baptism is "part and parcel of the total plan of God for His people."[33] Like Torrey, Tozer also highlights the *desire* to be filled as a key element. Both men also discuss that to be filled, you must *belong* to God. You must be a believer who has given your life to Christ.

Another evangelical-charismatic, Don Basham, also weighs in on how to be filled with the Spirit. In his book *A Handbook on Holy Spirit Baptism*, he recommends five steps:

1. Find a place for quiet prayer.
2. Reread the Scriptures where the Holy Spirit is promised.
3. Say a prayer of invitation to be filled. (This is similar to Torrey and Tozer's belief that one must belong to God and be ready to receive.)
4. Once the Holy Spirit is received, you will speak the language of the Holy Spirit.[34]
5. Continue walking in faith.[35]

Mary: In the Catholic Church, there is no official teaching on how to receive baptism in the Spirit, but there is helpful advice in one book I co-authored, *Baptism in the Holy Spirit* by International Catholic Charismatic Renewal Services.[36] To prepare for the baptism of the Holy Spirit, people need to receive clear preaching about God's personal, unconditional love for them. Often, inner healing is needed as well, since deep-rooted misconceptions about God and about ourselves can block us from fully receiving what God has for us. People need to be equipped with practical instruction about the gifts of the Spirit and how to use them, and about resisting the tactics of the evil one.

The best setting in which to receive baptism in the Spirit is within a group of brothers and sisters who have experienced it themselves and who will pray over you to impart this same gift. Many local churches offer such an opportunity through a Life in the Spirit Seminar, the Alpha course, Christ Renews His Parish, or similar programs. If you are hungry and thirsty to receive baptism in the Spirit, ask God for it, and *keep asking until your prayer is answered.*

God Will Do as He Pleases

While all the above suggestions can be helpful, we want to add a caution: Baptism in the Spirit must not be reduced either to a formula or to a theological position that has no correspondence to lived experience. The danger is that all the conditions or heart attitudes mentioned above could come to be considered prerequisites to experiencing the baptism in the Spirit.

Although these conditions are important, we must not let the grace of God be hemmed in by our conditions. We must always be open to the grace of God coming upon someone who is not seeking the baptism in the Spirit, even an unbeliever—even though it is not the normal operation of the Spirit, nor is it the normal order of salvation (cf. Acts 2:38). We have to shout with all our strength, "Ascribe power to God!" (Psalm 68:34). God is God, He is sovereign, and He can do what pleases Him.

Randy: I have seen God baptize people in the Spirit who were not seeking, not open and not asking for it. These people were either backslidden or carnal Christians at the moment they received it. As a pastor, I once asked God why He did this for a backslidden woman and for one of the most carnal men in my Baptist church, and why He did not do it for the head of the deacon board or for his brother, another deacon—both of whom were open and desirous of it. God's answer was that this was His way of fighting human pride and the tendency to turn His *charismata* (gifts of grace) into our *worksamata* (a made-up word meaning we receive gifts based upon our works or worthiness). This would cause us to lose our thanksgiving and praise for His work, substituting our own work in the place of Christ's work at the cross—moving from grace to works.

The woman I referred to considered herself in a backslidden state, having been out of church for months. She did not even know why she had come to the meeting the night she received the baptism in the Spirit. The carnal man was John Gordon. He, on the other hand, had been attending regularly and had been on the board of the church for several years. But the night before he received the baptism in the Holy Spirit, he realized that he had had a false conversion, and he was genuinely regenerated. He told me the next day, "I had been one of your disciples for years, but last night I became a disciple of Jesus."

When we began our healing seminar, John was against it. He was in the very back of the church, standing with his hand against the wall. When the speaker, Blaine Cook, gave the invitation, mentioned types of phenomena you might feel, and said to come forward if you did feel such phenomena, John said to himself, *That's a bunch of bull!*

You might say John was not open. But in spite of his opposition to the message, what he had just mocked started to happen to him. He was mightily touched by the power of the

Holy Spirit and came forward. He received a baptism in the Holy Spirit and began to flow in the gifts in a powerful way. He received especially strong gifts of word of knowledge, healing, prophecy and discerning of spirits, which enabled him to do deliverance ministry. Later, he received the gift of tongues for his devotional prayer life. No one in my Baptist church received a stronger gift than John did, yet he in no way met the criteria or conditions for receiving that we mentioned in this chapter.[37]

While in Europe, I met an apostolic leader's wife who had been raised as a secular Jew. Her first experience of Christian worship occurred in the woods, because the government had closed non-Orthodox church buildings. She had not heard the Gospel, and she was not a Christian. She asked a Christian lady who was worshiping in tongues, "What are you doing?"

The woman replied, "This is tongues."

The young Jewish woman replied, "It makes me feel good. I want it."

To which the Christian Pentecostal replied, "Oh, you're not holy enough to have this gift." (The Pentecostal lady did not know the young woman was not even a Christian.)

This secular young woman was apprehended by the Holy Spirit, who fell upon her, and she began speaking in tongues. This very unusual timing—the outpouring of the Spirit before conversion—was similar to the event in Cornelius's household in Acts 10, except there the baptism happened as they were hearing Peter preach. This young woman had not yet heard the Gospel when she was baptized in the Spirit and when God saved her. The two occurred simultaneously. She later was instructed in the Gospel.

A similar thing happened to a man in an Eastern European country, who told me his story the day after I heard about the formerly secular Jewish woman. I thought her story was bizarre, but when I heard this man's story, I realized God wanted to shake up my preconceptions regarding His sovereignty. The man had never heard the Gospel and he was not a Christian, but he had become interested in learning more about Christianity. He went to a street where Christians were worshiping. As he stepped into their midst, some were singing in tongues. He did not know what they were doing. Suddenly, the Holy Spirit fell upon him and he began to speak in tongues. He was taken to the leader of this group of Christians. The leader realized God had done something in this man that was quite out of the normal order, so he explained the Gospel to him, led him in a prayer of repentance and instructed him more fully. The man was baptized in the Spirit sovereignly prior to hearing the Gospel. The Pentecostal leader, like Peter at Cornelius's house, realized God had saved the man, so he caught him up on his understanding of what God had done to him. The leader accepted him and welcomed him into the fellowship of the church.

This man then gathered many of his family, neighbors and friends together and told them what had happened to him. He spoke in tongues in their presence and then asked, "Do you know what that means? It means the God who created the universe now lives in me! That is good news, and He would like to live in you." This is what the Pentecostal leader had told him. He then led several people to the Lord. By the time I met him, he had established the largest non-Orthodox church in his city. He had recently had a terminal illness that affected his brain, but he was healed of it.

———————

———————

These stories show that while the recommendations in this chapter are wise counsel and have helped thousands of people receive the baptism in the Holy Spirit, we have to avoid turning principles into laws. We must be open to the sovereign grace of God, who may do the unusual or the unexpected by touching and baptizing people in the Holy Spirit who have not met these conditions. We must be careful not to turn God's gift into a work of man, but must allow the grace of God in Jesus to be the bedrock upon which we approach the throne of God in our time of need.

Let's now look in the next chapter at what Paul teaches about the specific supernatural gifts that the Holy Spirit gives in order for Christians to fulfill their mission.

5

Revelation Gifts

To one is given the word of wisdom through the Spirit, and to another the word of knowledge according to the same Spirit . . . and to another distinguishing between spirits.

1 Corinthians 12:8, 10 NASB

The gifts of the word of wisdom, word of knowledge and discernment of spirits are often called revelation gifts because they depend on the Holy Spirit revealing what is known only to God.[1] Commentators differ on what precisely Paul meant by these three terms, but they are commonly used today in a way that is based on biblical principles as well as reflection on what God is doing now. Like the early Christians, who sought to understand God's will for the new Gentile converts in light of both Scripture and the present works of God, so Christians today seek to understand the gifts of the Spirit by studying both Scripture and the present works of God (see Acts 15:7–8, 12–18).

Although there are real distinctions between the gifts, it is wise not to overemphasize the distinctions. Often there is an overlap between gifts. One shades into another, and often two or more gifts are at work simultaneously. Let's look in more detail at Paul's teaching about each of these revelation gifts, as well as looking at some present-day examples of these gifts in operation.

Word of Wisdom

It is important to note that Paul is not speaking here simply of wisdom, but of a "word" (*logos*) of wisdom. He is referring to a specific insight from God that is applicable in a particular setting.

In the biblical understanding, wisdom is not merely theoretical and speculative. It is practical. It involves knowing how to live and act rightly, in a way that is pleasing to God. A word of wisdom, then, refers to supernatural wisdom given in the moment that leads a person to make the right decision, or reply with the right answer, or break through an impasse, or know what to do in a particular situation. It is a wisdom that has nothing to do with IQ and is not gained by human experience or learning, but is supernaturally given by God.

A biblical example of a word of wisdom is in Acts 10, when Peter received a vision of a sheet let down from heaven, filled with unclean animals, followed shortly afterward by a visit from some Gentiles. Peter was given supernatural wisdom to understand that this vision and visit meant that he was to show these men hospitality, go and enter the house of the Gentile Cornelius—something that was totally against his principles as a devout Jew—and preach the Gospel to them. His obedience to the leading of the Holy Spirit led to the first evangelization of Gentiles, a momentous step in the growth of the Church.

A word of wisdom for handling difficult situations (Randy)

When I went to speak at a well-known Christian university in the South, I did not know that one of the students was against the renewal that God had used me to birth in Toronto on January 20, 1994. I was just beginning the lecture when he asked me, "How do you know if this renewal is really of God or not?"

This was his opening salvo, followed by more attacks. I did not know he was disingenuous at the time. For some reason I said, "It all depends on your wife. B. B. Warfield was against healing. Jonathan Edwards, on the other hand, was open to manifestations because his wife was mightily touched with joy and laughter in the First Great Awakening. She would be so overcome by the Spirit that she would lose all strength and fall to the floor. The experience these men had in their homes affected how open they were."

The student never asked another question. Later, I found out that his wife was very supportive of the renewal, while he was against it. I did not know that, but all the members of the class did.

The word of wisdom for parents (Mary)

Parents are one category of people who very much need the gift of a word of wisdom! A friend of mine was a single mother raising a teenage son. She had returned to her faith and was growing in a personal relationship with Jesus. She knew she could rely on Him to help her raise her son, whose father was not around to model what it meant to be a man of God. One day, she was confronted with how much she needed God's help when she came home and turned on the computer, only to find the image of a naked woman filling the screen. She called her son, and, embarrassed, he admitted to using pornography.

Not knowing what to do, she told him, "Go to bed. We'll deal with it in the morning." She knew that if she simply disciplined him, he would just try harder to hide it from her next time. That night she got on her knees and prayed, *Lord, show me what to do!*

The Lord gave her a word of wisdom. The next morning she called her son, and after explaining to him why pornography is wrong, she said, "Here's what I want you to do: Write the life story of that woman whose image was on the screen. Use your imagination. I want to know who her parents were, how many brothers and sisters she had, where she lived, what her life was like, where she went to school and what she did with her friends. And most of all, I want to know what happened to her that caused her to so lose her dignity that she ended up posing for a camera that way."

Her son's jaw dropped. It was not what he expected. She made him write and rewrite the story until she was satisfied that he had a sense of this unknown female as a *person*. From that point on, he could never look at a pornographic image in the same way again.

Word of Knowledge

"Knowledge" in Scripture can refer to the knowledge of truths of the faith, such as the fact that our old self was crucified with Christ (see Romans 6:6), or it can refer to the knowledge of ordinary facts. The gift of the word of knowledge refers to a supernatural knowledge of facts that does not come through study, research, experience or any human means. Often, it involves knowledge of something God desires to do or is about to do in a particular situation.

Peter manifested this gift when he knew supernaturally that Ananias and Sapphira had lied about the proceeds of their property (see Acts 5:3, 9). Later, another Ananias, in Damascus this time, had a word of knowledge that Saul (Paul), the persecutor, had just been converted to Christ and was temporarily blinded, but would be healed by the laying on of hands (see Acts 9:8–12). While evangelizing in Lystra, Paul had a word of knowledge that a crippled man listening to him had faith to be made well. As soon as Paul declared the word, saying in a loud voice, "Stand upright on your feet!" the man sprang up and began walking (Acts 14:10).

The first letter of John says, "And this is the confidence that we have toward him, that if we ask anything according to his will he hears us. And if we know that he hears us in whatever we ask, we know that we have the requests that we have asked of him" (1 John 5:14–15). The key here is "according to his will." The word of knowledge is a means by which God makes us aware of what is according to His will in a particular setting.

The word of knowledge in evangelism (Mary)

Words of knowledge can be powerful tools for evangelization. My friend Father Mathias Thelen was on the phone one day ordering pizza for himself and some other priests. He struck up a conversation with the woman on the line, Emily, and the conversation began to turn toward God. Perceiving her openness, he began to share the Gospel with her by explaining that the essence of Christianity is to respond in love to the God who gave us His Son, Jesus.

As they were talking, an image came into Father Mathias's mind of Emily looking at herself in a mirror, with earrings on. He decided to take a step in faith and share it with her: "Even right now, as we speak, I see the Lord Jesus looking at you with love as you look at yourself in the mirror, with earrings on. The Lord wants you to know that He sees your beauty and delights in you, and that no matter what you've done in the past, He loves you and has a plan for your life."

There was silence on the line. Then he heard her trembling voice: "I feel as if I'm going to cry right now. How did you know that?"

"What do you mean?" he asked.

"Yesterday I had a terrible day, and life was so dim as I was thinking about the black hole I had fallen into in my past and about how I need to change my life. Then today, I put on the brand-new pair of earrings I just bought. Looking at myself wearing these new earrings made me feel better. How did you know? This is so amazing; I am blown away right now."

Father Mathias explained to her that Jesus knows her deepest struggles, that He wants to be part of her life, and that His love changes everything. Emily shared that she was a nonpracticing Protestant. But she was so moved by the conversation that she accepted Father Mathias's challenge to read a book about Jesus and consider coming back to church again. She was very excited.

As they were speaking, she suddenly broke in, "Oh no! Corporate is here, and I have to go."

He quickly responded, "Before you go, about the pizza . . ."

The word of knowledge for healing

Words of knowledge are used today especially in the ministry of healing. A word of knowledge can reveal a condition or pain that God wants to heal in a particular setting. If the person understands its purpose, the word causes a greater measure of faith to rise up, both in the heart of the one who received it and in the heart of the person it is for. Without understanding, however, a word of knowledge only creates curiosity.

Randy: Recently, I was in Brazil ministering in a Presbyterian church. I had taught on words of knowledge earlier in the week. I asked for members of the church who had never experienced this gift before, but for whom we had prayed for an impartation of the gift, to come to the front and call out what they thought God was revealing to them about a condition, a disease, a pain or some combination. About a hundred people came forward and gave what they thought might be from God. Mind you, they had never done this before in their lives. Ninety-nine were correct. Some of the people's words were very specific, naming the place the person in the congregation had pain, what the pain felt like, or the specific name of the disease. Several people were healed instantly, as soon as a word of knowledge was spoken. This often caused the person who gave the word to break down weeping as he or she saw someone instantly healed as a result of the word being given. Many of these healings occurred this way, as soon as the word of knowledge was given and before there was prayer for healing. That night, there were 1,100 healings reported in a crowd of about 3,500 people.

Very often, a word of knowledge works in relationship to the gift of faith: It either causes faith to rise up for the first time, or it increases the measure of faith. While ministering at a Baptist church in Rio de Janeiro, I received a word of knowledge by impression.[2] I thought of a man's name, Rinaldo or Rinaldi. I was not sure which way the name was pronounced; it was a subtle impression. Then I thought he would be a pastor, then that he had a child who needed to be healed, and finally, that the child was a daughter. When I gave the word, three men stood who had the name and who were all pastors. Two of them had children in need of healing, and one pastor had a daughter. I believed the word was for him. I asked him if his daughter was present. He said she was not. I asked him if she could come to the morning service the next day.

The next morning, he brought his seventeen-year-old daughter to the meeting for me to pray for her. When I interviewed them to find out what was wrong—in this case the word of knowledge had not revealed the nature of the problem—I found out that she had a rare disease in her fingers. The last joints of all her fingers were very dark from poor circulation; in fact, they were cold, and they were dying. The doctors did not know what was causing the problem or how to treat it. I prayed for her that morning. There was no indication of healing then, but by the evening service she was healed. I am sure the faith for this healing was created by the word of knowledge.

Another time, I was ministering in New Mexico. On this occasion, I had told the Lord that I would speak out any impressions I received because I thought I had been playing it too safe, and in doing so had missed many words of knowledge. The most prevalent way I had received words of knowledge was by feeling physical pain corresponding to a condition in someone whom the Lord wanted to heal. I wanted to grow in receiving words of knowledge through impressions.

While worshiping, I received five impressions. I did not understand how any of them could have been right. I even told the people, "I don't know if these last five words are really from the Lord, or if I am missing Him."

The words of knowledge were Artisian and artisan, seventeen staples, maritime accident (we were in the desert, and the people laughed when I gave that one), and crowbar. When I said the word *crowbar*, I prefaced it by saying, "I am almost certain this word isn't really from God, and that I am missing Him."

The words were all correct. There was an artisan from Artisia, the name of a small community I did not know existed; there was a person who had complications from surgery that involved seventeen staples; there was a pastor who had recently had an accident on a boat from which he was recovering; and there was a woman who had been beaten by her ex-husband with a crowbar. Her neck had been broken, her jaw had been broken, and she had lost her hearing in one ear. The amazing thing was that during worship she heard an impression, *I am going to heal you tonight of your crowbar issue. It is the heart you want healed rather than the physical, but I am going to give it to you anyway.* She was instantly healed emotionally and physically when I spoke the word *crowbar*. This caused her to know that it was not just her mind—her impression—that she was hearing. It truly was from the Lord. The word of knowledge created in her the gift of faith to receive emotional and physical healings.[3]

Growing in words of knowledge (Mary)

A couple of years ago, I was seeking to grow in the gift of words of knowledge. I had never used this gift in any significant way before, but I knew that it could be very effective in stirring up faith, especially faith for healing. In preparation for a prayer meeting I was going to lead one evening, I asked the Lord to give me some words of knowledge.

I received some very light impressions in my mind. I was not at all sure if they were from the Lord, but I decided to speak them out. So I said to the people in the prayer meeting, "I think the Lord has shown me that there is a man here who suffers from a skin condition and who also has same-sex attraction. The Lord wants you to know that He is healing you and strengthening you to be the man you were created to be in His image. Also, there is a woman here who has spent time in jail and is very ashamed of that. But the Lord says He is taking away your shame, and He has a plan for you to minister to other women in jail. Finally, there is someone here with pain in your left ankle, and the Lord is healing you."

Since some of these words were very personal, I told the people, "I will not ask you to identify yourself, but if you'd like to come to me afterward and tell me that one of these words was for you, it will build up my faith."

Afterward, not one, but two men came to me separately, both of whom had a skin condition and same-sex attraction, and both experienced great liberation through that word. Not one, but two women came to me separately, both of whom had spent time in jail and through that word felt a lifting of shame and a call to jail ministry. Curiously, no one came to say anything about a left ankle. But the next day, the prayer ministry team told me they had prayed over two people with pain in the left ankle, and in both cases the pain completely disappeared. The Lord gave me double for my trouble!

Discernment of Spirits

Discernment of spirits is a revelation from the Holy Spirit about the source of a particular thought, word or action—whether it originates from the Holy Spirit, from a demonic spirit or from the human spirit. This gift has multiple purposes. Sometimes it is connected to prophecy, much as tongues and interpretation of tongues have a complementary relationship. In this case, discernment of spirits helps the listeners, especially other prophets, to discern whether a message is truly from the Holy Spirit or not.

Another use of the gift is in recognizing when an evil spirit is at work in or with someone. Yet another use relates to distinguishing between noble purposes and ignoble purposes motivating someone's actions. In the latter case, it does not involve a demonic spirit, but a wounded or needy human spirit rather than a wholesome, healthy, mature human spirit.

A biblical example of this gift occurred during Paul's mission in Philippi, when a slave girl began to follow Paul and his companions day after day, crying out, "These men are servants of the Most High God, who proclaim to you the way of salvation" (Acts 16:17). What she said was doctrinally correct, but she was disrupting Paul's mission. Her cries may well have distracted or scared off the people he was trying to evangelize. Paul did nothing for several days, perhaps to make sure that his discernment was accurate. But finally, he "turned and said to the spirit, 'I command you in the name of Jesus Christ to come out of her.' And it came out that very hour" (verse 18).

Discernment of spirits to protect the sheep (Randy)

One time in my life as a pastor, I was concerned about a visitor to my church who started visiting the home groups in the church. I found out that he was using pseudoscientific language to hide what I thought might be occult practices that he was introducing to the new believers. I was suspicious, but I wanted to make sure before I confronted him about it.

One night as I was going to bed, my wife said from the closet, "I think I see something."

I replied, "What do you think you're seeing?"

She said, "I don't know. It's glowing—wait—I see hands around a glowing ball."

I asked her, "Do you have any idea what it means?"

She said, "No, I don't. Do you?"

I answered, "Yes." Then I told her what she did not know about—my concern about whether this man was involved in the occult. When I confronted him the next day, realizing that he might not know that what he was doing was wrong, I told him that he was welcome to remain in the church, but not if he continued these practices. I showed him from the Bible how what he was doing was an abomination to God. I was loving, but firm. I was the shepherd, and my job was to protect the sheep. He never returned.

The need for interpretation

It is possible to receive a genuine revelation from God and yet not interpret it rightly. This is why we need to use the revelation gifts with great caution, wisdom and sensitivity, knowing we are capable of making mistakes.

Randy: Years ago when I was a pastor, we had a visitation of the Holy Spirit. Shortly afterward, a friend of mine, John, received a powerful impartation of the Holy Spirit, including gifts of healing, words of knowledge and discerning of spirits. One night he was asleep, when all of a sudden he felt terrified and oppressed. He felt as if someone were trying to strangle him. He woke up and tried with great difficulty to call upon the name of Jesus. After a struggle he was able to do so, and the suffocating, strangling sensation immediately stopped, as did the great sense of fear. He was filled with peace and went into a vision. He saw the woman we were planning to pray for the next day, whom we had never met. In the vision, he saw her being raped when she was young. Only two close family members knew about it, and one had told her never to talk to anyone about it. The Lord showed him in the vision the name of the town in which she was raped, the name of the man who had done it and the kind of car in which it happened. Then he heard the word *adultery*. He also heard two names of demons.

The next day, I thought it best to connect to God prior to beginning the deliverance session. When we began to pray, we were about fifteen feet from this woman, who was seated in the front row of the church. She had lots of physical problems that caused her to have difficulty getting around, as well as psychological and spiritual problems.

The moment we began to pray, she fell off the seat onto the floor and began manifesting demons. John walked over to her and told her the man's name, the fact that she had been raped and the town in which it had happened. Her manifestations became stronger. She was screaming and hissing. He told her he knew about her adultery. She yelled that she had not committed adultery. My friend, who was only a few weeks old in these new spiritual gifts, believed he had heard God correctly, and insisted two or three times that she *had* committed adultery, because God had given him that word.

Then she yelled, "It wasn't me; it was my husband! I caught him with a young woman, and I wanted to kill the _____!"

John apologized, realizing he had received correct information, but had wrongly interpreted the revelation on this point. Everything else was correct. Then John commanded the two demons by their names, which he had heard in the vision. The demons left her.

Then John said to me, "Now, Randy, minister inner healing to her."

I did so, for quite some time.

She left healed. Her eyesight was greatly improved. She walked out carrying the walker she had needed to enter the church. She was also healed of terrible seizures.

This is just one example of John's strong gift of discernment. We would be driving on the highway, far from where we lived. When a car came up behind us, he would tell me that it would have a certain decal on the back associated with a secret society. He would be right. When I asked him how he knew that, he would reply, "When I get around the demonic, there is a twisting that starts in my muscles around my sternum." This was just one of the ways God worked discernment in John.

Growing in discernment of spirits

As with all the other gifts, it is possible to grow in discernment of spirits by taking steps in faith. Any revelation we think we have received from the Lord should be shared only with great sensitivity and respect for the person to whom we are ministering, allowing that person the freedom to either confirm or reject what we share.

Mary: My friend Dr. Tom Graves is a specialist in family medicine who has also been seeking to grow in the gifts. Recently, a patient who had suffered for years from anxiety and depression came into his office. These had ruled her life, and she was virtually paralyzed with fear. He had sent her to a psychiatrist, but when she came back for a recheck, she was still no better. Dr. Tom describes what happened on that visit:

> Then I heard the Holy Spirit speak to me. What I heard was shocking, and he prompted me to share it with her. But I did not want to. After wrestling with Him for a while, I shared with her what I heard: I did not think her anxiety was medical, but rather, there was something very frightening and painful from her childhood that she had buried for many years.
>
> The woman's eyes filled with tears, and she said, "I just want to leave that part alone. It doesn't matter anymore."
>
> I told her I knew that she had been raped by someone she loved—someone who was supposed to protect her.
>
> She started crying and admitted this was true. She said, "But it doesn't matter; I never see that person anymore."
>
> I told her that God said that today we would defeat Satan and his demons, if she was willing. I said this fearing, *What if the prayer doesn't work?*
>
> But I felt God telling me He was going to act. I asked her if she was willing to trust Jesus and pray. She agreed, so we prayed right there in the office. As we prayed God's blessing, I told her I saw a beam of light shining directly from the heart

of our Father in heaven directly into her heart. And then I actually felt a *pop* and she was released.

The person she had brought along to our appointment said, "Did you feel that?" All three of us could feel it at the same time.

I know it sounds strange, but God did a miracle. Her face was completely calm, and her frown was replaced with a smile. I taught her how to pray this prayer by herself when the evil one tried to attack her again. She was a patient who had always stressed me out because I could never accomplish anything meaningful for her. Now, she is finally able to be loving and at peace. I think this is a sign of the times that we are moving into.

————

Now we have taken a close look at the revelation gifts—the word of wisdom, word of knowledge and discernment of spirits—and have seen how the Holy Spirit reveals through them things known only to God. Next we will examine the power gifts—the gift of faith, gifts of healing and the working of miracles—to see how vividly they demonstrate God's power to move in every situation.

6

Power Gifts

To another [there is given] faith by the same Spirit, to another gifts of healing by the one Spirit, to another the working of miracles. . . .

1 Corinthians 12:9–10

The gifts of faith, healing and miracles are called power gifts because they vividly demonstrate God's power over disease, demons, death and every destructive force. A gift for casting out demons, which Jesus said would accompany those who believe in Him, also fits in this category (see Mark 16:17).

The Gift of Faith

The spiritual gift of faith is different from the saving faith in Christ that is the foundation of the Christian life. The gift of faith is an unshakable conviction given by God that He is going to act supernaturally in a particular situation. Jesus speaks of this gift when He says, "Have faith in God. Truly, I say to you, whoever says to this mountain, 'Be taken up and thrown into the sea,' and does not doubt in his heart, but believes that what he says will come to pass, it will be done for him" (Mark 11:22–23). The Greek wording of verse 22 literally says, "Have *faith of God.*" It is a faith that cannot be produced or stirred up by any human effort, but is a pure gift of God. In 1 Corinthians 13:2 Paul speaks of the same gift as "faith, so as to remove mountains."

How does God give this kind of faith? Often, it is through prophecy or words of knowledge, which communicate His desire for the specific accomplishment of His will in a particular setting. God's revelation of His will causes all doubt to flee from the mind and creates the ability to believe that what He revealed is truly going to happen.[1] This communication, coupled with "the confidence that we have toward him, that if we ask anything according to his will he hears us" (1 John 5:14), creates a cause and effect in the Kingdom of heaven, and the result is the releasing of God's power for healings or miracles.

Randy: Here are two examples of miracles that came through the gift of faith. I was ministering in an Evangelical Presbyterian church, conducting a healing seminar one night a week for about ten weeks. During that time, I met a Methodist woman who told me she was going to have to have her carotid arteries reamed out to prevent a stroke. Several weeks later, while I was at home, my carotid artery started throbbing. It was very noticeable. When it happened, I was thirty-two and had never had anything like this happen to my artery. I knew it was a word of knowledge for this older lady. On the way to the town where the meetings were held, my other carotid artery started doing the same thing. I told everyone in the car that God was going to heal this lady. That night, I met her at the door and declared to her that God was going to heal her. I did something that night I had never done before. I stopped the worship and told everyone that God was going to heal this woman right now. In front of everyone, I spoke to her arteries and told them to be reamed out. I spoke healing to them. She was noticeably touched. You could see the arteries throbbing in her neck. She was healed and did not have to have the surgery. This kind of bold faith, where there is no doubt, was not something I worked up, but a gift God worked in me.

Once when I was ministering in Uberlandia, Brazil, a young woman had terminal cancer. It had metastasized and was in all the organs in her abdomen, her breasts and her bones. The doctors had operated, but when they saw where all the cancer had spread to, they did not remove any of the tumors. They just sewed her back up and told her she had only a few months to live. When I prayed for her, I saw none of the usual signs of God's presence for healing, such as tingling, trembling, heat, electricity or peace. (Or sometimes, if there is a strong infection that causes heat, one sign might be a cold feeling where the person had been hot from the infection.) Yet I believed with all my heart that she was going to be healed—so much so that I prayed for her for twenty minutes without anything happening. I just kept telling her I did not care if she believed or not; I had enough faith for both of us, and God was going to heal her. Which He did.

What caused such strong faith on my part? While I was on my way to pray for a line of about fifty people, the woman's friend, who had brought her to the meeting, told me that she had had a dream in which she was told that if she would have the man whose name was on the opposite side of a coin she was given pray for her friend, the friend would be healed. When she turned the coin over in the dream, it had my name on it. This friend had never heard of me. But the next day or so, while traveling through a city, she saw my name on a billboard related to healing. Hearing this gave me the faith to believe—to know—that her friend was going to be healed. It caused the gift of faith, and I had no doubt. I was convinced she would be healed.

The Gifts of Healing

The gift of healing is God's supernatural action to bring a sick person to physical, emotional or spiritual health. Paul literally speaks of this gift in the plural, "gifts of healings" (1 Corinthians 12:9), since there are many different kinds of healing. Healing is not something we can do in our own strength or ability. It is done by God's power, which comes as a gift through our faith and prayer. When we pray for people, laying hands on them, and nothing happens, we see what we can do. On the other hand, when the person is healed, we see what God's energy can so powerfully do through us (see Colossians 1:29).

Jesus put special emphasis on healing in His missionary instructions to His disciples—and there is no indication that He has changed those instructions since then!

He sent them out to proclaim the kingdom of God and to heal.

Luke 9:2

And they departed and went through the villages, preaching the gospel and healing everywhere.

Luke 9:6

The Lord appointed seventy-two. . . . And he said to them, ". . . Whenever you enter a town and they receive you . . . heal the sick in it and say to them, 'The kingdom of God has come near to you.'"

Luke 10:1–2, 8–9

Go into all the world and proclaim the gospel to the whole creation. . . . And these signs will accompany those who believe: . . . they will lay their hands on the sick, and they will recover.

Mark 16:15–18

The reason healings are so important for evangelization is that they are not just an external proof of the Gospel. They are the *embodiment* of the Gospel. They visibly demonstrate the fact that the Kingdom of God is here and that Jesus has come to free human beings from sin and all its destructive effects, as well as to restore us to the fullness of life. They are signs of the fullness of healing that will be accomplished on the last day, when our bodies will be raised from the dead to share in God's own life forever.[2]

Breakthrough in healing (Randy)

I have spent the last 47 years in ministry. I believed in healing because God called me into ministry about a month after I was healed of terrible injuries from a car accident. I occasionally prayed for healing during the first 14 years of my ministry, and I may have seen 5 people healed. Then after an impartation for healing, when someone laid hands on me and prayed for healing anointing to come upon my life, I began to see healings much more frequently, perhaps on a monthly basis. If there was an intention to conduct a service just for healing, I saw healing almost every time. This continued for about 8 years. Then after another time of impartation, there was a much greater anointing for healing. Healing seemed to be occurring on a weekly basis.

I experienced another increase in healing after a 40-day fast in which I ate nothing solid, neither any soups nor broths, but I drank juices and water. This was my second 40-day fast; my first had been for a breakthrough in healing. The purpose of this second fast was to seek God in prayer and fasting for an increase in anointing in order to see miracles, not just healing. Before this fast I had been confronted with children and teenagers who needed creative miracles, none of whom had been healed. It was heart-wrenching. On the 23rd day of the fast, I experienced my first creative miracle. A creative miracle is when God restores a limb, organ or tissue that was missing completely from a person's body.

In January 1995, I experienced a major breakthrough in healing. It was not following a time of fasting, and it was not related to a time of impartation. I had been in ministry for 25 years. Unexpectedly, while ministering in a renewal meeting in Melbourne, Florida, a greater anointing for healing came upon my life. It continued later in the same month in North Carolina. During that month, I saw more healings than during the preceding 25 years combined. This new level of grace on my life for healing continued for about 4 years, where we averaged 3 percent of the crowd being healed in every service where we prayed for the sick.

Then, during a series of renewal meetings at Bethel Church in Redding, California, I had another breakthrough. I saw 137 healings in one meeting, when normally I would have seen 30. After this night, instead of seeing 3 percent of a crowd healed, I would see 10 percent. And if the presence of God was stronger in the meeting, the percentage would jump to 20 or 30 percent, or occasionally higher. The greatest number I have seen healed to date was 90 percent in a meeting of 11,000 people in Manaus, Brazil.

On-the-spot healings (Mary)

Sometimes the Lord does the most remarkable healings when we are not looking or planning for them. My friend Dan Almeter is a leader of Alleluia Community, an ecumenical charismatic community in Georgia. He and a friend were giving a retreat at a parish. After Mass they went to the church hall for a potluck, and during the meal they happened to mention that they prayed for people for healing. Dan recounts what happened:

> As soon as we finished talking, people started coming up to ask for prayer. The first to get in line was a lady in her sixties who could barely walk even with her walker. She was almost in tears with the pain. She explained that six months earlier, she had fallen and broken her hip in three places. Surgeries had not helped at all.
>
> So we prayed over her, and when we finished, we asked if she would take our hands and try to stand up. She reluctantly did so, expecting to experience pain, but there was none.
>
> We then asked her to let go of her walker, take our hands and take a few baby steps. We promised not to let her fall.

Again she was very reluctant, but she obeyed. She took a few steps and starting saying, "Oh my gosh! Oh my gosh!" Then her hands went up in the air, and she started to praise the Lord.

The next thing you know, she was literally running around the room, totally pain-free, weeping and praising God. About six months later I saw her again, and she said she had never had another problem with her hip.

The Working of Miracles

The working of miracles is when God uses us to effect a miracle by His divine power. The New Testament word for miracle is *dunamis*, which literally means a mighty deed or deed of power—something that goes beyond any human explanation. Scripture is full of God's miracles, but the gift of miracles refers to God partnering with one of His children, as He loves to do, to work a miracle through that person's faith and prayer.

The working of miracles often depends on an understanding of the ways of God. Moses said to the Lord, "If you are pleased with me, teach me your ways so I may know you and continue to find favor with you" (Exodus 33:13 NIV). A little later, Moses said, "Now show me your glory" (verse 18). The key to a life of miracles is becoming more aware of the "ways of God."

Miraculous healings (Randy)

The gift of faith is important for operating in the gift of miracles. While ministering at a Messianic congregation in a city on the Black Sea in Ukraine, we saw three miraculous healings in one night. The first was an elderly Jewish man who was a Holocaust survivor. He came in a wheelchair, having been unable to walk for some years. During the time of ministry, there was a word of knowledge for the man. He attempted to stand in response to the word. When he did, he was healed. Later that night, he accepted Yeshua (Jesus) as his Messiah.

That same night, a mother asked me to pray for her fourteen-year-old son, who was completely deaf in one ear. I prayed for him and Jesus healed him. I was excited to see a deaf ear open, but the mother did not think I was excited enough. I told her that I had seen other deaf ears open before.

She replied, "Yes, but have you ever seen a deaf ear healed when there was no auditory nerve?"

I was shocked. I asked her, "What do you mean?"

She told me, "Our doctor here told us that tests indicated that my son's auditory nerve had been destroyed. We're not sure how it was destroyed, but perhaps by a high fever. He recommended we go to Venice, Italy, to see another specialist. We did, and he confirmed that my son's auditory nerve was missing."

When I heard this, I was more excited! This was not a healing where some part of the body in a diseased state was restored to health. It was a creative miracle.

A third healing miracle that occurred in that congregation was also connected to a word of knowledge. While ministering, I had a mental picture. I saw a tractor that was pulling a sickle behind it. This piece of equipment has a long blade that is used to cut the grass to make hay. When it is being transported down a highway, its blade flips up over the machine and is locked in place. In this vision I saw that it was almost dark. The tractor was coming around a curve. The driver did not realize that the blade had come loose and was sticking out about five feet beyond the pavement. As the tractor was coming around a curve, I saw two teenage girls walking. When the tractor passed them, the blade hit one girl close to the knees. It was a terrible accident, almost amputating her legs. This mental picture lasted only a few split seconds. It was not an open vision, but more of a mental picture, like a daydream.

I thought to myself, *That would be a better word of knowledge if this meeting were being held on a collective farm, rather than in this large city. The likelihood of the word of knowledge being right would be higher.*

I realized that the only way I could know for sure if this was an accurate word from God was to give it—and to risk looking like a fool if I was wrong. I shared the word just as I had received it. On the back row was an older woman who stood up immediately and was healed right then. There was not even a prayer for her, because the word created a gift of faith in her to believe she was going to be healed. She came forward and told us her story. Everything in my mental picture word of knowledge had been correct. Her legs had almost been amputated. As a result, for the next forty or fifty years of her life, she had not been able to walk properly. She could not bend her knees. When she came to a staircase, she had to turn around and swing her stiff legs to the right or left since her knees would not bend. She showed us how she had had to navigate stairs. Then she walked up the stairs normally for us. She showed us how she could bend her knees. The friend with whom she had come was overcome with joy for her friend's healing.

Another creative miracle occurred in Fortaleza, Brazil. A 25-year-old man had been born without the optic nerve being connected to the back of his eye. He had become quite successful and had gone to a specialist to see if anything could be done to restore sight to his eye. The specialist said, "There is nothing we can do to heal your eye. If you ever see out of that eye, it will be a miracle of God."

This young man came to our meeting. Two of my friends, Steve Wilson and Ed Rocha, prayed for him. His eyesight was restored. This impacted the young man's family so profoundly that they sold their homes and business to move from the north of Brazil to Fortaleza. Friends of the family converted to Christ as a result of this miracle.[3]

During the meetings in Fortaleza, a teenager was healed of total deafness. It was really interesting how it happened. She was seated off to the right, where she could not see the team who were giving words of knowledge. She had been born stone-deaf in both ears, unable to hear anything. A member of my team gave a word of knowledge about a right ear. When this word was given, the young deaf girl, who obviously could not have heard the word and who was seated in a place that prohibited her from seeing the team, suddenly began to put her hand on her ear and indicate to her mother that her ear had opened up and she was hearing.

A few seconds later, another team member gave a word of knowledge for the other ear. Instantly, the girl began to place her hand over her other ear, once again motioning to her mother that her ear had opened up and she could hear.

When we realized something had happened and a commotion was beginning where she was seated, we went to her and found out her story from the mother. Her father was there as well. He was in shock. He told us her story without emotion, matter-of-factly. By the time he and his daughter made it through the crowd to the stage, however, his shock was over and he was an emotional mess as he tried to tell the audience what had happened to his daughter, who had been born deaf and had never heard a sound before.

Another creative miracle occurred recently in Brazil. Once again, it involved a young woman who had been born stone-deaf. She, too, had never heard a sound. Late in the evening, someone brought her onstage to be prayed over for healing. Several people, including myself, were praying for her hearing. For quite some time there was no sign anything was happening. Then she began to hear out of her right ear, but it was very little. She could not hear a snap of the fingers, or a voice, but when I began to clap my hands within a few inches of her ear she could hear it. We all were excited about the beginning of her healing. Through the next several hours, we continued to pray for her healing. Gradually, we could clap farther and farther away from her ear and she could hear it. We finally had to quit due to the lateness of the hour, well past midnight. When we quit praying, she could hear voices, different pitches, hands clapping and fingers snapping. Since she had never heard a sound, however, she could not repeat anything we were saying.

The next morning, this girl was awakened by the sounds of the pots and pans in the kitchen, and by the sound of a dog barking outside her window. She did not know it was a dog, but one of the members of the family had heard the dog barking, found a video on his cell phone of a dog barking and played it for her. She smiled and communicated through sign language that this was the sound that had woken her up. She came to our service that morning at a different church. She told her testimony through sign language, which her mother interpreted. At the end of the service, I saw her praying in sign language for another young person who was deaf. We had to leave, so I don't know if the other young person was healed.

Both of these young women experienced not only healings, but also creative miracles, because they were born stone-deaf, with parts of their ears missing.

During one of my earlier trips to Brazil, we were ministering in a church in Uberlandia. It was a large church, with hundreds of people coming to Christ each month. Two men on my team were praying for a six-year-old little girl who had worn braces on her legs her whole life. While they were praying, one of the men had an impression that they were to ask the mother for permission to take the braces off the girl's legs. They did.

The mother said, "If you do, she will fall on the floor. She can't stand without the braces."

One of the men replied, "I believe we are to take her braces off and God will heal her." Then the mother agreed. When they took the braces off, the little girl did not fall to the floor but began to run all over the platform.

As exciting as it was to see this little girl running with such joy, I was shocked to hear the rest of the story. The mother told us, "There is more to this story than you realize. When you first came to this church six years ago, I came to you with a picture of my daughter as a newborn. I had taken the picture in the hospital after I was told she had died, and that there was no brain activity; she had flat-lined. I brought her picture to you and asked you to pray for her. You did pray, and when I returned to the hospital, she had come back to life. So she was not only healed in her legs today, but she was raised from the dead six years ago.[4]

Food multiplying (Mary)

Several times a year, my friend Butch Murphy takes teams on a mission to a garbage dump outside Mexico City, where thousands of people survive by combing through the garbage for plastic bottles, cans and other items they can sell. The teams offer food, medical care, prayer, catechesis and Bible study. On several occasions, Butch has witnessed what he can only explain as a miraculous multiplication of food.

One day the team had brought large garbage bags, each filled with food staples that would not need refrigeration and could last a long time—rice, dried pasta, bottled water, condensed milk, sugar and salt. The team had been able to put together 412 bags to distribute, one per family. On this day there were mobs of people, so Butch and the team did what they often do: They knelt down, along with the local people, and laid hands on the food. They gave thanks to God, then specifically asked God to multiply the food. When the crowds are large, the team sometimes will stop halfway through the distribution and pray all over again. On that day, over 600 people went through the line. (The coordinators, who line the people up in groups of 50, counted them.) Every person got a bag of food.

Another time, when the team consisted of young adults, they were giving out ham-and-cheese sandwiches, with a piece of fruit and a bottle of water. Butch recounts what happened:

> We had the sandwiches in cardboard boxes, and José, our friend down there, was wrapping them in napkins and giving

them out to people. As the line kept coming, he said, "Do you have any more sandwiches?"

I went into the bus and looked on all the seats. I looked under the seats, I looked above, I walked up and down the bus, and there were no more sandwiches.

José pulled out his jackknife and started cutting sandwiches in half. He said, "All we can do now is trust the Lord."

At that moment, a kid came up to me with a box of sandwiches and said, "Hey, Butch, were you keeping these sandwiches for something, or are we supposed to hand them out?"

I asked, "Where'd you get those?"

He said, "They were sitting on the front seat of the bus."

José started crying and pointed up to the heavens, saying "Gloria a Dios!" He put away his knife and started handing out whole sandwiches.

Just then, someone else came up and elbowed me. "Hey, Butch, we got these boxes of apples. Are we supposed to hand them out?"

I asked, "Where'd you get those?"

"They were on the front seat of the bus."

Two or three times, people kept coming off the bus with things from the front seat. There were enough sandwiches and fruit for everyone.

Such miracles, small and great, are part of the great river of God's mercy that is flowing through His Church in our time, and overflowing to a world that is desperately in need of Him. In the next chapter, we'll look at the gifts of speech—tongues, interpretation of tongues and prophecy—which often work in conjunction with the power gifts by helping people understand who God is and what He is doing, and to praise Him in return.

7

Gifts of Speech

To another [is given] prophecy . . . to another various kinds of tongues, to another the interpretation of tongues.

1 Corinthians 12:10

What then, brothers? When you come together, each one has a hymn, a lesson, a revelation, a tongue, or an interpretation. Let all things be done for building up.

1 Corinthians 14:26

The gifts of prophecy, tongues and interpretation of tongues are loosely grouped together because they all involve speech—whether in a human language or in a language known to God alone. A Spirit-inspired hymn composed during a time of worship, an anointed teaching or a revelation (a deeper insight into God and His plan) also belong to this category of gifts.

Prophecy

Prophecy is speaking a message inspired by the Holy Spirit, especially for the "upbuilding and encouragement and consolation" of others (1 Corinthians 14:3). Paul regards prophecy as exceptionally important because of its power to build up the Church. It is the only gift that appears every time he lists the charisms.[1] A prophetic word can build up by arousing people's faith, deepening their understanding, stirring them to worship or piercing their hearts with conviction of sin (see 1 Corinthians 14:24–25). It is striking how often Paul exhorts Christians to strive for this gift:

> Earnestly desire the spiritual gifts, especially that you may prophesy.
>
> 1 Corinthians 14:1

> The one who speaks in a tongue builds up himself, but the one who prophesies builds up the church. Now I want you all to speak in tongues, but even more to prophesy.
>
> 1 Corinthians 14:4–5

> Earnestly desire to prophesy.
>
> 1 Corinthians 14:39

> Do not quench the Spirit. Do not despise prophecies, but test everything. . . .
>
> 1 Thessalonians 5:19–20

Prophecy is distinct from teaching in that teaching usually involves a prepared and organized presentation, but prophecy is a spontaneous message directly inspired by the Holy Spirit. Because it is from God, prophecy has the power actually to bring about that which it proclaims—whether conviction, or counsel, or consolation or comfort. It releases God's revelation into the present context.

Prophecy comes in many different forms. A prophetic word can be specific guidance from the Holy Spirit. For instance, it was a prophecy that launched Paul and Barnabas on their first evangelistic mission (see Acts 13:1–3). It may be in the form of visions or dreams. Ananias, Paul, Cornelius and Peter all had visions.[2] Joseph, the foster father of Jesus, had no less than four prophetic dreams that gave him specific instructions (see Matthew 1:20; 2:13, 19, 22). The Magi also had a prophetic dream (see Matthew 2:12).

Prophecy may include the reading of hearts—that is, God revealing the secrets of a person's heart, usually to convince the person that He is real and that He knows and loves him or her. It is important to note that God will not reveal the secrets of a person's heart to anyone who will misuse this information.

Prophecy can include recognizing what is invisible to the eye. Anna the prophetess and Simeon recognized that the infant Jesus, who must have looked like an ordinary baby being brought into the Temple by His parents, was the Messiah (see Luke 2:25–38). A prophecy sometimes foretells the future, such as Agabus's word that there would be a famine, and that Paul would be arrested and handed over to Gentiles (see Acts 11:28; 21:10–11).

More often, prophecy is not a prediction, but a "now word" from God, speaking God's revelation into the present situation in a way that encourages, instructs and strengthens those who hear it. Throughout Acts, it is evident that prophecy was part of the normal life of the Church.

Ever since the end of the apostolic age, prophecy does not give any new revelation to add to what God has already revealed in Christ (as, for instance, Mormons believe happened with the prophecies Joseph Smith supposedly received). Rather, it makes God's unchanging revelation in Christ come alive for the present generation. Prophets have the ability to make God's people come alive spiritually—to put skin and flesh on dry bones and fill dead bodies with the life-giving breath of the Spirit (see Ezekiel 37:4–13).

Mary: An example of a prophetic word that brings encouragement was given by someone at my parish, Christ the King, in Ann Arbor, Michigan, at the Vigil Mass[3] of Pentecost 2017:

> As we began to worship in Mass, I saw in the Spirit water flowing from the base of this altar, running down the steps. I saw water begin to fill this place ankle-deep, then knee-deep. Then I saw the Spirit of God come into our hearts in a very profound way and begin to flood us. I felt that the Lord was saying, *I'm sending a flood of My Spirit. I'm filling you with My Spirit in a new way, and you are that flood that I am sending out to cover this land, to cover the Church, to cover nations, to cover the world.* The Lord wants us to continue to open ourselves up to that flood— not a flood that brings destruction, but a flood that brings healing and new life, that flows over the land and turns what is parched and desert into a land that is green and brings new life.

The value of prophecy

Paul makes a distinction between tongues and prophecy: Tongues is spoken to God, but prophecy is spoken to people.

He insists that the reason prophecy is so valuable is that the message is understandable to those who hear it.

> Pursue love, and earnestly desire the spiritual gifts, especially that you may prophesy. For one who speaks in a tongue speaks not to men but to God; for no one understands him, but he utters mysteries in the Spirit. On the other hand, the one who prophesies speaks to people for their upbuilding and encouragement and consolation. The one who speaks in a tongue builds up himself, but the one who prophesies builds up the church. . . . The one who prophesies is greater than the one who speaks in tongues, unless someone interprets, so that the church may be built up.
>
> 1 Corinthians 14:1–5

In verses 9–11, Paul further elaborates on this principle:

> If with your tongue you utter speech that is not intelligible, how will anyone know what is said? For you will be speaking into the air. There are doubtless many different languages in the world, and none is without meaning, but if I do not know the meaning of the language, I will be a foreigner to the speaker and the speaker a foreigner to me.

This principle means we must prophesy in such a way that the message makes sense. Prophecy is communicating a revelation from God, and revelation means the making known of what was hidden. If a prophecy is given in such a way that it cannot be understood, then it cannot edify, encourage or comfort those to whom it is given. A practical application is that when giving a prophecy to someone who has little biblical knowledge, we need to avoid using "Christianese," and instead use plain language that person can understand.

Prophetic evangelization

Paul emphasizes the evangelistic power of prophecy, especially in the form of reading hearts: "If all prophesy, and an unbeliever or outsider enters, he is convicted by all, he is called to account by all, the secrets of his heart are disclosed; and so, falling on his face, he will worship God and declare that God is really among you" (1 Corinthians 14:24–25). Many unbelievers have come to Christ through Christians speaking prophetically to them. In these situations, prophecy often overlaps with a word of knowledge.

Mary: My friend Patrick Reis was invited to speak to kids at an inner-city adolescent center. After a meal with the students, who were mostly nonreligious, he shared his testimony of how he had encountered Jesus and had become His disciple. He then offered to pray with any students who were hungry for God. A junior high boy named Jayden came to him, and Patrick asked God to share His heart and desires for Jayden's future. At that moment, the Lord showed Patrick images of Jayden scared and afraid while walking on the streets. He then saw God desiring to release heavenly protection over him and take away the fear in his life.

Patrick said to Jayden, "The Lord told me that you have a lot of fear when you walk on the streets."

Before Patrick could say anything else, Jayden gasped, overwhelmed. Patrick went on to say, "God does not want you to live in fear, and He's going to protect you on the street with angels. He's going to take away the spirit of fear and give you a spirit of power, love and a sound mind."

As Patrick spoke those words, Jayden experienced the presence of God, was filled with the Holy Spirit and praised God.

The next day, the director of the center asked Patrick to meet with Jayden in her office. The boy looked at Patrick and asked, "How did you know that walking on the streets is my biggest fear?"

Patrick said, "God told me that about you because He wants to show you that He knows you and that He loves you so much. You're never alone, but always protected!"

Later that day, Jayden told everyone in the group about his encounter with God, and soon afterward he joined a Catholic youth group.

Prophesying with love and respect

A prophecy should always be given with an attitude of love and respect for those to whom it is addressed. In the case of a prophetic word to an individual, the word should be said in a tentative way rather than a dominating way. For instance, you can begin with, "I think the Lord is saying this . . ." and end with, "Does that make sense to you?" It is also important to keep in mind that a prophecy involves not only a revelation from God, but also its proper interpretation and application. It is possible to get the revelation right, but interpret or apply the word wrongly.

A personal word that involves correction should normally be given only to someone you already have a relationship with—a person who trusts you enough to receive the word. When real prophets give a word of correction, the result is that the person is edified, not condemned. If you think you have received a word of correction for someone, it is good to pray, *Lord, You wouldn't show me that unless You wanted to help this person, or set this person free. What do You want me to do with this word so that it can build this person up?*

Can everyone prophesy?

In his Pentecost sermon, Peter explained to the crowd what God had just done in pouring out His Holy Spirit (see Acts 2:14–36). His message was, in essence: "This outpouring of the Holy Spirit is the crowning moment of Jesus' whole mission—it is what He died and rose to give us! It is what the patriarchs prayed for, what the prophets prophesied, and what the psalmists sang about. It is the fulfillment of God's promises!" Significantly, Peter began his sermon by quoting an Old Testament passage that is all about prophecy:

> But this is what was uttered through the prophet Joel: "And in the last days it shall be, God declares, that I will pour out my Spirit on all flesh, and your sons and your daughters shall prophesy, and your young men shall see visions, and your old men shall dream dreams; even on my male servants and female servants in those days I will pour out my Spirit, and they shall prophesy."

> Acts 2:16–18

In the Old Testament, the Holy Spirit came upon certain people who were specially chosen to be prophets—people such as Moses, Miriam, Elijah, Isaiah and Jeremiah. But in this passage from Joel, God promised that one day there would be a universal outpouring of the Spirit on His whole people—men and women, young and old, slave and free. The coming of Christ was not to bring an end to the gift of prophecy, but rather, to extend it to all God's people. Peter proclaims the fulfillment of this promise. The Holy Spirit makes the Church into a community of prophets. This does not mean that all have the spiritual gift of prophecy, which is a particularly effective and stable ability to prophesy (see

1 Corinthians 12:29). But all have the capacity to prophesy, speaking under the inspiration of the Holy Spirit.

Paul reaffirms the fact that prophecy is a gift available to all believers: "For you can all prophesy one by one, so that all may learn and all be encouraged" (1 Corinthians 14:31). Again, this does not mean that all believers actually do prophesy, since many are not aware of this gift and do not know how to activate it or grow in it.

Growing in the gift of prophecy

Learning to use the gift of prophecy well is a growth process, as is true with all the gifts. The more you practice, the more you grow. If a one-year-old baby were constantly worried about using bad grammar or saying the wrong thing, he or she would never learn to talk! Whoever tries to walk in the gifts of the Spirit will make mistakes, but mistakes can be the occasion for further growth. A key to this process is to be humble and not to take yourself too seriously.

A good way to begin growing in the gift of prophecy is to listen to the Lord's voice for your own life. Jesus said, "My sheep hear my voice" (John 10:27). Hold what you think the Lord is saying to you in your heart, write it down in a journal and go back to read it from time to time. As we steward the prophetic words that God has already given (either to us as individuals or to a whole community) by reflecting on them, praying about them and taking steps in accord with them, He is able to take us further.

Another way to open yourself to prophecy is to be immersed in the Word of God, so that your mind is renewed by it. Each of the biblical prophets had read and studied earlier prophets. Jeremiah, for instance, was familiar with the words of Isaiah. Ezekiel in turn studied Jeremiah. If a prophet assimilated the revelation God had already given, God could use him to bring further revelation.

Tongues

The gift of tongues is speech inspired by the Holy Spirit in a language the speaker does not understand. In First Corinthians, Paul seems to speak about two different forms of this gift: tongues as a language for personal prayer and praise, and tongues as a public message for the congregation.

Tongues as a gift for prayer, praise and worship

Tongues as a prayer language is a means by which the Holy Spirit enables a person to praise and thank God, uninhibited by the need to conceptualize or put into words the movements of the heart. It is like a musical composition without lyrics. Paul refers to this form of the gift when he writes, "For one who speaks in a tongue speaks not to men but to God; for no one understands him, but he utters mysteries in the Spirit" (1 Corinthians 14:2). It is a gift for expressing our love for God in a way that overflows beyond the limitations of human language. Prayer in tongues bypasses the mind and comes directly from the heart; it is thus a form of what Catholic tradition calls contemplative prayer—a kind of prayer in which the mind is not active, but the heart is completely attentive to God. One of the most beautiful forms of this gift is when a whole congregation is singing in tongues together, in a rising and falling harmony inspired by the Holy Spirit, worshiping God as with one voice.

Tongues as a prayer language is the only spiritual gift that Paul specifically notes is not for the benefit of others, but rather, benefits the one using it: "The one who speaks in a tongue builds up himself" (1 Corinthians 14:4). It edifies us by deepening our relationship with the Lord and enkindling our love for Him. To edify yourself is a very good thing since it gives you a greater capacity to edify others in turn.

Tongues as a public message

The gift of tongues in the second sense, as a message for the Church, fulfills its purpose only when it is followed by an interpretation. It then becomes a form of prophecy. This second form of the gift is much more rare than the first.

Paul emphasizes that whoever gives a message in tongues should pray for an interpretation, so that people can understand it and be built up by it. Otherwise, it has no value. He writes, "One who speaks in a tongue should pray that he may interpret" (1 Corinthians 14:13), and "The one who prophesies is greater than the one who speaks in tongues, unless someone interprets, so that the church may be built up" (verse 5).

Tongues as a gift for intercession

The gift of tongues can help us in praying for others. Paul may be referring to tongues when he speaks of the inexpressible groanings of the Spirit:

Likewise the Spirit helps us in our weakness. For we do not know what to pray for as we ought, but the Spirit himself intercedes for us with groanings too deep for words. And he who searches hearts knows what is the mind of the Spirit,

179

because the Spirit intercedes for the saints according to the will of God.

Romans 8:26–27

When we are not sure how to pray for a person or situation, especially in the case of a seemingly impossible situation, tongues can help us become attuned to what God wants to do. Our prayer then becomes much more effective. Sometimes as we pray in tongues, the Lord may give us a specific sense of how to focus our prayer. At other times, we are simply praying in union with unutterable groanings of the Spirit.

Paul also exhorts us to "pray in the Spirit on all occasions with all kinds of prayers and requests" (Ephesians 6:18 NIV). To "pray in the Spirit" probably refers to praying in tongues, as well as other forms of Spirit-inspired prayer. Another possible reference to tongues is in Jude 20–21: "But you, beloved, building yourselves up in your most holy faith and praying in the Holy Spirit, keep yourselves in the love of God . . ."

Randy: In 1984, when my oldest was about three years old, while suffering an asthma attack he said to his mother, who was praying for him, "Mommy, don't pray that way; pray the other way."

My wife, DeAnne, responded, "What do you mean, Josh?"

He replied, "You know, Mommy—when you use the words I don't understand."

My wife asked, "Why, Josh?"

He told her, "Because, Mommy, it works better."

Now, my three-year-old did not have any theology to prove or disprove. Yet I have always been amazed by this dialogue and by Josh's perception of what kind of prayer helped the most.

In 1994 or 1995, I experienced my first creative miracle when a woman's brain was restored from advanced Parkinson's disease. When I contacted my wife to tell her about the miracle, she said, "It happened about midnight last night, didn't it?"

I responded, "Yes. How did you know?"

She told me, "About midnight Jeremiah [who was under two years old] woke up screaming with an earache. All I could do to get him to stop screaming was to pray in tongues over him. If I prayed in English, he continued to scream in pain, but when I prayed in tongues, he would stop. I had to pray all night, until about 5:00 a.m. I felt as though this was a counterattack, and that you must be having a powerful healing or miracle."

I do not want to diminish the power of prayer in English or in any human language, but I want to report my wife's experience faithfully. I don't have a theology to support here, or anything more than the telling of an unusual testimony that relates to a way tongues can be helpful to us in our lives.

The miraculous gift of tongues

God sometimes uses the gift of tongues in a more obviously supernatural way, where the person is able to speak in a human language that he or she has never learned. This form of the gift is called xenolalia. On the day of Pentecost, the manifestation of tongues had this miraculous character:

> And they were all filled with the Holy Spirit and began to speak in other tongues as the Spirit gave them utterance.
> Now there were dwelling in Jerusalem Jews, devout men from every nation under heaven. And at this sound the

multitude came together, and they were bewildered, because each one was hearing them speak in his own language. And they were amazed and astonished, saying, "Are not all these who are speaking Galileans? And how is it that we hear, each of us in his own native language? Parthians and Medes and Elamites and residents of Mesopotamia, Judea and Cappadocia, Pontus and Asia, Phrygia and Pamphylia, Egypt and the parts of Libya belonging to Cyrene, and visitors from Rome, both Jews and proselytes, Cretans and Arabians—we hear them telling in our own tongues the mighty works of God."

Acts 2:4–11

Luke does not make clear whether the miracle was of *speaking* or of *hearing*. Were the disciples speaking in languages they had not learned, or were they speaking in unintelligible sounds that the listeners miraculously heard in their own languages? Either way, God used this miracle of communication to astonish people and open their hearts to the Good News of Christ that Peter was about to preach.

Randy: I have a friend in Mozambique who speaks twelve or fourteen languages. He told me that some of these languages are similar to one another, but others are as different from each other as English is from Russian or Korean. He would go into a new area to evangelize and would hear the language, and he would be given the ability to speak it and understand it. There are many stories of people speaking in such languages, including a few that I have witnessed. This is the less common experience, however, both in the Bible and today.

Mary: God sometimes uses the miraculous gift of tongues to convince people of the supernatural power of the Holy Spirit. Some years ago, there was a priest from Uganda visiting my parish. He was skeptical of the charismatic gifts, but one day he was on the altar at Mass as the whole congregation was praying in tongues. He was astounded to hear another priest behind him, a native of Michigan, begin praising God in his tribal language of Uganda. He turned and asked him, "How did you learn my tribal language?" When the other priest assured him that he had no knowledge of African languages and was just praying in tongues, the visitor became convinced of the reality of this gift.

Like other speech gifts, tongues sometimes works together with gifts of healings or miracles. One time, a friend of mine was serving as pastoral associate at a parish, and she got a call from some parishioners, who asked her to go to a local hospital's ICU to pray with a family member, Seoun, who was on life support. My friend asked if they wanted a priest, but they said no, because this person was estranged from the church due to an incident with a priest years ago. My friend recounts,

> I drove there immediately, praying in tongues on the way for God to give me words of comfort and welcoming.
>
> I arrived at the ICU and was met by Seoun's husband. He walked me into the ICU, where Seoun was hooked up to life support, seemingly lifeless. He explained that she had had a massive stroke. He was scared and didn't know what to do.
>
> I joined hands with Seoun and invited her husband to pray with me. Immediately, tongues came. For me, it was a tongue I wasn't familiar with. Seoun began to move, and her eyes began to flutter. The ICU nurses came on the scene and asked if we could vacate the room. Clearly, something was occurring, and it wasn't clear whether Seoun was taking a turn for the worse or the better.

As we walked to the waiting room, her husband asked me where had I learned Seoun's native tongue, Korean. He said it was perfect Korean, and what I was praying was Seoun's childhood prayer to Jesus.

My response was "Praise God!"

The husband confided in me about their anger at the church, and we prayed together for them to be delivered from it. Clearly, God was there to touch each of them. Then the nurses came and got us. Seoun had awoken and was responding to touch, and they were amazed!

A few weeks later, Seoun was able to visit the parish in a wheelchair and thank me personally for the prayer. Now, years later, Seoun enjoys a vibrant life. Both she and her husband had returned to their faith, and I was awakened to just how much God loves His people!

Tongues in Church history

Tongues is the gift that, more than any other, many assume disappeared from the life of the Church for some seventeen hundred years (from around AD 200 to AD 1900). But, in fact, tongues never completely disappeared; it only became less common. As we mentioned in chapter 3, the church fathers often spoke of this gift by using the term *jubilation*. Later in Church history, this gift is easily recognizable in the writings of various saints.

Saint Bernard of Clairvaux, a twelfth-century monk who rekindled fervor and holiness in the Cistercian order, writes of praising God in a way that goes beyond rational thought:

> But if at times, when the heart expands in love at the thought of God's graciousness and mercy, it is all right to surrender our mind, to let it go in songs of praise and gratitude, I feel

that I have opened up to the Bridegroom . . . not a narrow lattice but a wide-open window. Through it, unless I am mistaken, [God] will look with greater pleasure the more he is honored with the sacrifice of praise.[4]

Saint Thomas Aquinas, one of the keenest intellects in history, was also a man of the heart when it came to prayer and praise. He speaks of praying aloud, but without words:

When our mind is kindled by devotion as we pray, we break out spontaneously into weeping and sighing and cries of jubilation and other such noises. . . . We have to serve the God to whom we offer reverence in prayer not only with our minds, but also with our bodies.[5]

The jubilus is an inexpressible joy which is not able to be expressed in words but even so the voice declares this vast expanse of joy. . . . the things that are not able to be expressed are the good things of glory.[6]

Saint Teresa of Avila, a sixteenth-century nun who re-formed the Carmelite order, not only prayed in this way, but also desired that all her fellow nuns would do so:

Our Lord sometimes gives the soul feelings of jubilation and a strange prayer it doesn't understand. I am writing about this favor here so that if He grants it to you, you may give Him such praise and know what is taking place. . . . It seems like gibberish and certainly the experience is like that, for it is a joy so excessive that the soul wouldn't want to enjoy it alone but wants to tell everyone about it so that they might help this soul praise our Lord. I knew a saint named Friar Peter of Alcantara . . . who did this very thing, and those who . . . listened to him thought he was crazy. Oh what blessed madness, sisters! If only God would give it to us all![7]

Saint John Vianney was a nineteenth-century French priest who was renowned for his simplicity and holiness. He was conversant only in French. One woman who went to him for confession and asked his advice about what God wanted for her reported,

> Monsieur Vianney spoke as if to himself, for the space of five minutes and in a tongue unknown to me; at any rate I could not understand him. In my astonishment I looked into his face. He seemed to be out of himself, and I thought that he beheld the good God.[8]

Growing in the gift of tongues

Tongues as a language for prayer and praise is the simplest and most widely distributed of all the gifts of the Spirit mentioned in 1 Corinthians. As with the other gifts, Paul encourages Christians to seek this gift: "Now I want you all to speak in tongues, but even more to prophesy" (1 Corinthians 14:5). Clearly, the gift of tongues is not obligatory, and no one should make it a standard for whether someone is a real Christian or not. On the other hand, it comes highly recommended by the apostle Paul, whose advice carries some weight. He models a balanced perspective: Tongues is a wonderful gift, but prophecy is even better. "I thank God that I speak in tongues more than all of you," Paul wrote. "Nevertheless, in church I would rather speak five words with my mind in order to instruct others, than ten thousand words in a tongue" (1 Corinthians 14:18–19).

Many people are afraid of tongues because of its oddness. Indeed, the very idea of adults making unintelligible sounds can seem offensive to the intellect. Yet for this very reason, tongues can teach us to hand over control to the Lord. To speak in tongues requires a willingness to become like a child—to look foolish or feel foolish for Christ. Many people find that tongues becomes a doorway to other gifts of the Holy Spirit because it gives us practice in yielding to the Spirit without being completely passive.

There is a widespread misunderstanding—partly due to scholars who have analyzed the biblical texts without ever having seen this gift in operation—that to speak in tongues is to be in a kind of religious ecstasy where people lose control of themselves. But that is not normally the case. A person who speaks in tongues remains fully in control and can stop or start at will, yet there is a real surrender to the Holy Spirit. It is like driving a car: To maneuver the car, you need to both press the gas pedal and turn the steering wheel. To begin praying in tongues, you need to begin making sounds (pressing the gas pedal), but then let the Holy Spirit take over (letting Him turn the steering wheel). As we let Him take over, our tongue becomes more fluid. In most cases, whoever asks for this gift perseveringly and begins "pressing the gas pedal" receives the gift.

Interpretation of Tongues

Interpretation of tongues is a gift that always operates together with a public message given in tongues. It is a supernatural ability to understand the message and to proclaim it in a language understood by the listeners, so that all can be built up by it. It is not a direct translation, but an interpretation of what was said.

Paul teaches, "If any speak in a tongue, let there be only two or at most three, and each in turn, and let someone interpret" (1 Corinthians 14:27). The one who interprets may be the same person who spoke in tongues, or may be someone else. The message in tongues may even be in the form of song, and may be interpreted by someone in an interpretation that is itself sung.

When an interpretation comes forth, it is a kind of prophecy. Why, then, did there need to be a message in tongues in the first place? A message in tongues can have a powerful effect on the listeners. It speaks to the heart rather than the mind, and it focuses attention on the Lord's majesty and transcendence. The interpretation that follows then has greater impact.

Discerning Prophecy and Other Gifts

Paul teaches that the exercise of prophetic gifts must be discerned: "Let two or three prophets speak, and let the others weigh what is said" (1 Corinthians 14:29). The fact that a prophet is inspired by God does not mean he or she is infallible. Even if a word comes from God, it comes *through* the prophet and thus can be influenced by human thinking or human interpretation.

Scripture also contains many warnings against false prophets. Jesus said, "Beware of false prophets, who come to you in sheep's clothing but inwardly are ravenous wolves" (Matthew 7:15). Later He added, "For false christs and false prophets will arise and perform great signs and wonders, so as to lead astray, if possible, even the elect. See, I have told you beforehand" (Matthew 24:24–25).[9]

Following are some basic biblical criteria for discerning prophecy. These criteria can also be applied to the use of other spiritual gifts.

1. The truth test

Prophecy and all gifts that involve revelation must be in full accord with truth, since the Holy Spirit cannot contradict Himself. This means that prophecies should be weighed to discern whether they are consistent with Scripture, and, for Catholics, with the teachings of the Catholic Church.

> Now concerning spiritual gifts, brothers, I do not want you to be uninformed. You know that when you were pagans you were led astray to mute idols, however you were led. Therefore I want you to understand that no one speaking in the Spirit of God ever says "Jesus is accursed!" and no one can say "Jesus is Lord" except in the Holy Spirit.
>
> 1 Corinthians 12:1–3

Paul is giving a very simple rule of discernment. No matter how inspired a person may seem, if he or she says something false or contrary to the Christian faith, it is not from the Holy Spirit. The first and second letters of John provide a similar doctrinal test:

> Beloved, do not believe every spirit, but test the spirits to see whether they are from God, for many false prophets have gone out into the world. By this you know the Spirit of God: every spirit that confesses that Jesus Christ has come in the flesh is from God, and every spirit that does not confess Jesus

is not from God. This is the spirit of the antichrist, which you heard was coming and now is in the world already.

1 John 4:1–3

For many deceivers have gone out into the world, those who do not confess the coming of Jesus Christ in the flesh. Such a one is the deceiver and the antichrist.

2 John 1:7

Scripture teaches that God created everything good, including the material world. But in the ancient world, there were widespread philosophical views that denigrated the material world and regarded the body as unworthy or even evil. For this reason, some Christians were tempted to deny the reality of Christ's incarnation. But John makes the belief in the incarnation of Christ the very touchstone of Christian faith, and thus a basic doctrinal test of prophecy.

2. The love test

Any authentic prophecy contributes to building people up in love. Paul underscores this essential criterion in his chapter on love, 1 Corinthians 13, which is at the very center of his teaching on the spiritual gifts in chapters 12 through 14:

If I speak in the tongues of men and of angels, but have not love, I am a noisy gong or a clanging cymbal. And if I have prophetic powers, and understand all mysteries and all knowledge, and if I have all faith, so as to remove mountains, but have not love, I am nothing. If I give away all I have, and if I deliver up my body to be burned, but have not love, I gain nothing.

1 Corinthians 13:1–3

Paul's statement is stark: Prophecy or any other charism, no matter how spectacular, is absolutely worthless without love.

The love test does not mean that every prophecy will be about comfort and affirmation. True prophecies are not always feel-good messages. Some are a call to repentance or a warning of judgment. A prophecy that brings conviction or warning, however, should never be judgmental, but must always be given in love and in solidarity with those who hear it. Even a stern word can have a powerfully edifying effect if the speaker is motivated by genuine love for God's people. At a large ecumenical conference in Kansas City in 1977, Ralph Martin gave this prophecy:

> Mourn and weep, for the body of my Son is broken.
>
> Come before me with sackcloth and ashes, come before me with tears and mourning, for the body of my Son is broken.
>
> I would have made you one new man, but the body of my Son is broken.
>
> I would have made you a light on a mountaintop, a city glorious and splendorous that all the world would have seen, but the body of my Son is broken.
>
> The light is dim. My people are scattered. The body of my Son is broken.
>
> Turn from the sins of your fathers. Walk in the ways of my Son. Return to the plan of your Father, return to the purpose of your God.
>
> The body of my Son is broken. . . .[10]

People all over the stadium began weeping as they heard this prophecy and were deeply convicted by the Holy Spirit regarding the scandal of disunity among Christians. Today, more than forty years later, people still talk about this prophecy.

3. Giving glory to Christ

Any true prophecy or other spiritual gift gives glory to Jesus Christ, focusing attention on Him rather than on the individual using the charism. Using a spiritual gift is a way of honoring God, as Peter teaches: "As each has received a gift, use it to serve one another, as good stewards of God's varied grace . . . in order that in everything God may be glorified through Jesus Christ" (1 Peter 4:10–11). Whether we are giving a prophecy, or ministering healing, or using any other gift, it is important to keep turning people's attention to Jesus and help them recognize that He is the source of the power. After Peter had healed the lame man at the Temple gate, he told the crowd where to aim their amazement: "Why do you stare at us as if by our own power or godliness we had made this man walk? . . . It is Jesus' name and the faith that comes through him that has completely healed him" (Acts 3:12, 16 NIV).

Sometimes charisms, especially the more sensational ones, can lead to an unhealthy tendency to put people on a pedestal. To Paul and Barnabas's dismay, they experienced this after they healed a crippled man in Lystra. The next thing they knew, the citizens of Lystra were acclaiming them as gods and preparing to offer sacrifice to them. Paul and Barnabas had to take immediate and strong action to forestall such idolatry:

> They tore their garments and rushed out into the crowd, crying out, "Men, why are you doing these things? We also are men, of like nature with you, and we bring you good news, that you should turn from these vain things to a living God, who made the heaven and the earth and the sea and all that is in them."
>
> Acts 14:14–15

Peter had to respond in a similar way when the centurion Cornelius fell at his feet in reverence: "But Peter lifted him up, saying, 'Stand up; I too am a man'" (Acts 10:26). The key to ensuring that the use of gifts is Christ-centered rather than me-centered is to pray often for humility—and to know that the Lord will arrange circumstances in your life to answer that prayer effectively!

4. *Good order*

No matter how true a prophetic word is, it will not bear good fruit if it is not in harmony with what the Lord is already doing in the present context. Prophecies can be authentic and yet be given in a time or circumstance where they are unhelpful, or even harmful. Like the slave girl who followed Paul in Philippi, shouting acclamations, they can be doctrinally correct but disruptive to the work of God. Paul gives this rule: "So, my brothers, earnestly desire to prophesy, and do not forbid speaking in tongues. But all things should be done decently and in order" (1 Corinthians 14:39–40).

We have to be careful not to overapply this rule, however. Sometimes the Holy Spirit bursts the "old wineskins" of our plans, our structures or our ideas of what God can and cannot do. The gifts of the Spirit are often marked by an unexpectedness or even strangeness that upsets our complacency. We have to have a spirit of openness and be ready to shift gears in response to the Spirit's leading, as Paul did on his missions when the Holy Spirit prevented him from going where he planned and then led him in a completely new direction (see Acts 16:6–9).

5. Good fruit

Jesus gave us this principle: "Beware of false prophets. . . . You will recognize them by their fruits. Are grapes gathered from thornbushes, or figs from thistles? So, every healthy tree bears good fruit, but the diseased tree bears bad fruit" (Matthew 7:15–17).

We are to look for good fruit in the life of a prophet or other spiritually gifted person, although sometimes it takes time for the fruit to become visible. The fruit the Lord looks for is not measurable in human terms. Scripture speaks of two different kinds of fruit. Paul describes the fruit of the Spirit as dispositions of *being*: love, joy, peace, patience, kindness, goodness, faithfulness, gentleness and self-control (see Galatians 5:22–23). And Jesus speaks of the fruit of *doing* the kinds of works that He did—such as healings and miracles—in the authority of His name (see John 15:1–16).

Who discerns the spiritual gifts?

Who is responsible to discern a prophecy or other gift? The first gateway of discernment should be the person using the charism. If I have a word of prophecy, I need to check it against my knowledge of Scripture and the teachings of the Church. I need to consider whether it will truly build people up in love or whether it could tear down, whether it is in good order, and so on.

Second, since no one is always able to perfectly discern his or her own gifts, discernment is exercised by pastoral leaders in the immediate setting—for instance, the leaders of a prayer meeting, worship service or conference—with the help of other prophets.

Finally, the ultimate responsibility for discernment, especially in the case of a prophecy that raises major pastoral questions or has repercussions beyond the immediate setting, belongs to the pastors or leaders of the church. For Catholics, this refers to the parish priest or ultimately the local bishop.

To discern is not to squelch

Paul indicates that the role of leaders in regard to spiritual gifts is to discern them and coordinate their interaction for the good of the Church (see Ephesians 4:11–13). But he strongly cautions that pastoring the gifts does not mean suppressing them: "Do not quench the Spirit. Do not despise prophecies, but test everything; hold fast what is good. Abstain from every form of evil" (1 Thessalonians 5:19–22).

This implies that heavy-handed leadership can, in fact, quench the Holy Spirit, as in putting out a fire. Leaders may be tempted to "despise prophecies." Why? Perhaps because prophesying does not conform to well-laid human plans. People learning to use the gift of prophecy may make mistakes that need correction. Its exercise in a congregation may require careful discernment and guidance (as in the Church in Corinth). Leaders can find it all too easy to suppress the gifts instead of pastoring them wisely. Again Paul cautions, "Earnestly desire to prophesy, and do not forbid speaking in tongues. But all things should be done decently and in order" (1 Corinthians 14:39–40).

His principle is simple: Do not hinder the manifestations of the Spirit, but test them and ensure they are being used appropriately. We are not to quench the fire of God, but fan it into flame! (see 2 Timothy 1:6).

Saint John Chrysostom, a fourth-century church father, gave similar advice:

> The most basic task of a church leader is to discern the spiritual gifts of all those under his authority, and to encourage those gifts to be used to the full benefit of all. Only a person who can discern the gifts of others and can humbly rejoice at the flourishing of those gifts is fit to lead the Church.[11]

8

Activating
the Spiritual Gifts

If this book has stirred up in you a desire to let the Holy
Spirit manifest His supernatural power more freely through
you, know that the Lord desires it more than you do. His
will is for His Church to be "clothed with power from on
high," fully equipped with gifts from heaven that enable us
to manifest God's love, presence and power in this world. It is
a tragedy that vast numbers of Christians have no idea what
the charisms are or how to use them, causing the Church in
some places to look like more a weary widow than the radi-
ant bride of Christ. On the other hand, where Christians in
large numbers are using the spiritual gifts, the Church looks
like what she truly is: the bride of the risen Lord Jesus, the
One who has triumphed over death and has been given all
authority in heaven and on earth.

In this concluding chapter, we offer twelve keys that we
have found helpful for activating and growing in the spiritual

gifts. It is important to keep in mind that using the gifts is not a matter of mastering a skill, since the gifts do not function by human power, but by the Holy Spirit's power operating through us. It is always God alone who is in control. But it is possible to open ourselves more fully to God's action.

1. Be Filled with the Holy Spirit

Jesus told His apostles, "You will receive power when the Holy Spirit has come upon you" (Acts 1:8). The gifts that supernaturally empower us to do God's work flow from receiving the Giver Himself, the Holy Spirit. As we mentioned in chapter 1, the gifts are not like tools you can keep in your pocket to pull out whenever you feel like it. They are God the Holy Spirit acting in and through you. So the first key to using the gifts is to be filled with the Holy Spirit.

Even if you have already received the Holy Spirit through faith and baptism (and for Catholics, confirmation), there is always more. A traditional theological principle is that whatever is received is according to the capacity of the receiver. The Holy Spirit, being God, is infinite, but our capacity to receive Him is limited. There is always infinitely more of Him than we have received already, and our capacity for Him needs to expand continually. This is why many traditional prayers to the Holy Spirit include the verbs *come* and *fill* us. These prayers teach us to invite the Holy Spirit more fully into our lives.

One of the most powerful means of receiving more of the Holy Spirit and His gifts is by an impartation of the Spirit through prayer and the laying on of hands.[1] This is not referring to a sacrament, but to the simple biblical gesture of laying on of hands, as Ananias did for Saul (see Acts 9:17). Many people who previously did not move in certain gifts begin to do so after they are prayed for and receive an impartation of the Spirit, some with the laying on of hands, and others without it.

Even after receiving an impartation of the Spirit, we have to remain radically surrendered to Him. Part of what makes the spiritual gifts so valuable is that they force us to be dependent on the Holy Spirit. We cannot manufacture even the tiniest genuine healing or prophecy or word of knowledge out of our own resources. We can only cooperate with what the Holy Spirit desires to do through us. (It is true that the gifts can be counterfeited, but the counterfeits are spiritually fruitless and usually easy to spot.) So we have to live in continuous reliance on the Spirit. "If we live by the Spirit, let us also keep in step with the Spirit" (Galatians 5:25).

2. Stay Close to Jesus

The Holy Spirit is the Spirit of Jesus (see Romans 8:9), and everything He does in us is Christ Himself acting through His Spirit. It follows that the more united we are to Jesus, the more freely He is able to work through us. Luke reveals this secret when he describes the reaction of the Jewish leaders to the apostles' preaching: "When they saw the boldness of Peter and John, and perceived that they were uneducated, common men, they were astonished. And they recognized that *they had been with Jesus*" (Acts 4:13, emphasis added). On one level, this simply means that Peter and John were recognized as disciples of Jesus. But on a deeper level, people sensed that there was something extraordinary in the courage and authority of these men—something that went beyond any human explanation and could only be explained by their closeness to Jesus.

It is "being with Jesus" in the intimacy of a personal relationship that allows us to be instruments of His love and power. To be with Jesus is like spending time near a nuclear reactor—you cannot *not* be changed by it. The more deeply united we are with Jesus, the less we try to accomplish things by our own puny efforts, and the more He is able to radiate His divine power through us. He is the source of all fruitfulness in using the gifts. "I am the vine; you are the branches. Whoever abides in me, and I in him, he it is that bears much fruit, for apart from me you can do nothing" (John 15:5).

For the apostles, "being with Jesus" was not just a temporary, three-year phase that they graduated from after He died, rose and ascended into heaven. A literal translation of Acts 4:13 is *"they were* with Jesus." Even after His resurrection and ascension, they were still with Him. They maintained their connection to Him through daily prayer, worship, studying His words, studying the Scriptures, celebrating the Lord's Supper (the Eucharist) and fellowshiping in the Christian community (cf. Acts 2:42–43).

In the same way for us, "being with Jesus" has to be renewed day by day, by entering into His presence through praise and worship (and for Catholics, through Eucharistic adoration); by studying His Word; by listening to Him and getting to know His voice; by repenting whenever we sin; and by letting Him heal us, purify our motivations and cut out of our lives all that is not of God. All this is not our work, but a work of the Holy Spirit in us that we surrender to: "For it is God who works in you, both to will and to work for his good pleasure" (Philippians 2:13).

3. Get God's Heart for the Lost and Broken

Being an instrument of God's power is closely connected with receiving God's heart. God gives us a share in His power not so we can do whatever we feel like doing, but so we can do the things that are on His heart. If we are not in tune with His heart, we can pray for many things with little effect.

In the gospels it is easy to see what is on God's heart. Jesus had a special love for people who were in desperate need—either because they were sinners estranged from God or because they were sick, disabled, marginalized, lonely, troubled or outcast. Often, before Jesus performed a healing or miracle, the gospels tell us that He was "moved with compassion" for the needy person in front of Him.[2] It was His compassion that released His healing, liberating power.

Jesus summed up His whole mission by saying, "The Son of Man came to seek and to save the lost" (Luke 19:10). In some church circles, it has become unfashionable to talk about "the lost." To have God's heart, we have to acknowledge the biblical truth that there are people who are lost. They are not necessarily bad people, but they are living apart from God, alienated from Him (see Colossians 1:21). Some, even including many baptized Christians, are in deep moral and spiritual darkness. God weeps for these lost sons and daughters, and He longs to bring them home to His fatherly embrace.

One of the biggest obstacles to being used by God is simply indifference. We may feel some compassion when we see hurting or lost people, yet it does not compare to the infinite fire of God's compassion for them. The more we share in God's heart, the stronger will be our desire to be a conduit of His love and mercy. But there is a cost to letting go of our indifference: It means letting our own hearts be broken with God's compassion. Paul wrote to the Corinthian Christians, "I will most gladly spend and be spent for your souls" (2 Corinthians 12:15). For him, that meant not only grueling travels and ministry, but also shipwreck, stoning, the lash, constant danger, hunger and thirst. We can only say this with Paul and really mean it if we have been captivated by Jesus and are letting our hearts be transformed by His.

4. Ask, Seek, Knock

Many people are not sure it is even legitimate to ask God for the gifts of the Holy Spirit. But Jesus went to great lengths to convince us that we should ask God confidently for good things, especially for the Holy Spirit and His gifts:

> Ask, and it will be given you; seek, and you will find; knock, and it will be opened to you. For everyone who asks receives, and the one who seeks finds, and to the one who knocks it will be opened. Or which one of you, if his son asks him for bread, will give him a stone? Or if he asks for a fish, will give him a serpent? If you then, who are evil, know how to give good gifts to your children, how much more will your Father who is in heaven give good things to those who ask him!
>
> Matthew 7:7–11

In Luke's version of this passage, the last phrase is "how much more will the heavenly Father *give the Holy Spirit* to those who ask him!" (Luke 11:13, emphasis added).

Jesus also said, "Again I say to you, if two of you agree on earth about anything they ask, it will be done for them by my Father in heaven" (Matthew 18:19). And again, "And whatever you ask in prayer, you will receive, if you have faith" (Matthew 21:22; cf. Mark 11:24). In these scriptural promises and admonitions to pray, we have a solid foundation to believe it is good to ask God for the spiritual gifts, even being specific about which gifts we desire to experience in our own lives.

Paul, too, insists that there is nothing wrong in asking for great things from God for the sake of our mission to be Christ's witnesses in the world. On the contrary, it is wrong not to ask! "Earnestly desire the higher gifts . . . earnestly desire the spiritual gifts, especially that you may prophesy" (1 Corinthians 12:31; 14:1). When it comes to the gifts of the Spirit, we have not asked for too much, but too little. And we have not expected too much of God, but too little. As Saint Teresa of Avila said, "You pay God a compliment by asking great things of Him." To ask great things of God is an act of faith, believing that He is capable of great things. "He who did not spare his own Son but gave him up for us all, how will he not also with him graciously give us all things?" (Romans 8:32).

Scripture gives us another important principle about asking. Jesus said,

> Truly, truly, I say to you, whoever believes in me will also do the works that I do; and greater works than these will he do, because I am going to the Father. Whatever you ask in my name, this I will do, that the Father may be glorified in the Son. If you ask me anything in my name, I will do it.
>
> John 14:12–14

What does it mean to ask "in Jesus' name"? It does not mean just to use His name as a formula, ending a prayer with "in Jesus' name, Amen." The sons of Sceva found that out, to their dismay, when they tried to cast out a demon in Jesus' name and instead were attacked and overcome by the demon (see Acts 19:13–16). They were not Jesus' disciples and were not acting in union with Him or according to His will.

Rather, to ask in Jesus' name is to ask on His authority, which He shares with those who are in Him. The more we do so, the more God delights in displaying the power of Jesus' name before the world.

5. Take Steps in Faith

The apostles said to Jesus, "Increase our faith!" (Luke 17:5). They were hoping He would answer, "Okay, I will increase your faith." But instead, He told them to *act on* whatever faith they had, no matter how small: "If you had faith like a grain of mustard seed, you could say to this mulberry tree, 'Be uprooted and planted in the sea,' and it would obey you" (verse 6). As the healing evangelist John Wimber used to say, "Faith is spelled R-I-S-K." It is by actually exercising faith—by taking risks—that our faith increases.

When the prophet Elijah was about to be taken up to heaven, he encouraged his young disciple, Elisha, to ask for whatever he wanted. Elisha's response was bold: He wanted a "double portion" of Elijah's spirit—his supernatural gifting for prophecy, signs and wonders. Elijah answered, "You have asked a hard thing; yet, if you see me as I am being taken from you, it shall be so for you, but if you do not see me, it shall not be so" (2 Kings 2:10). Elisha did indeed see Elijah as he was taken up in a whirlwind—the sign that his desire was granted. But the key to Elisha's being launched into prophetic ministry was that he immediately took a risk in faith, doing just what he had seen his master do: He struck the water of the Jordan with Elijah's mantle. The water parted, and he crossed over on dry ground (see verse 14). He went on to perform many healings and miracles, just as Elijah had done. He received what he asked for—a double portion.

In a similar way, Jesus' disciples *saw* Him as He ascended into heaven, and then they were filled with His Holy Spirit at Pentecost. Peter and the other apostles immediately began to take risks in faith: proclaiming the works of God in tongues, preaching the Gospel boldly and saying to a man lame from birth, "In the name of Jesus Christ the Nazarene, walk." And the disciples who were being baptized into the Church were being truly discipled to do what Jesus had commanded the Twelve and the seventy-two to do: heal the sick, cast out demons and raise the dead. Acts 4:29–31 tells us that all who received the power of the Spirit were enabled to speak the word boldly—exactly what the Church had prayed. Then, when the Church was scattered due to persecution following Stephen's martyrdom, the "hand of the Lord" was with them (Acts 11:21). "Them" does not refer to the apostles, who remained in Jerusalem, although surely the hand of the Lord was with them, too. But "them" is a reference to the laity being used supernaturally by the Spirit as they flowed in His gifts. (The wall between the clergy and the laity needs to be removed when it comes to moving in God's power.)

Mary: I vividly remember the first time I took a big risk in faith. I had just returned from a two-week mission in Brazil with Randy's team. I was speaking at a Catholic conference in the Middle East, and I knew the Lord was asking me to step out in faith for healing in a way I never had before. It truly felt like jumping off a cliff, since I had no idea what would happen or whether anything would happen at all. I named several specific physical conditions, asked people who had those conditions to stand up, and then had everyone in the congregation pray a simple prayer for them. After the prayer, I had to leave the stage quickly because it was the next speaker's turn.

To my amazement, the speaker came up to the podium in tears and said, "I've had hearing loss in one ear ever since I was hit by a soccer ball several months ago, and when you prayed, 'Ears, be opened in the name of Jesus,' my ear popped open. Now I can hear fine!"

That event brought my faith to a new level.

6. Do Whatever He Tells You

At the wedding of Cana, Jesus' mother gave us another secret to walking in the supernatural gifts of the Spirit. She said to the servants, "Do whatever he tells you" (John 2:5). These words, the last that Mary speaks in the gospels, resound to all Christians of all time.

In the context of that wedding, Jesus had not yet done any miracles. His public ministry had not begun. Mary noticed that the wine had run out—symbolic of God's people lacking the true "wine" of divine life, the Holy Spirit. She brought this need to her Son.

Surprisingly, Jesus responded with an apparent refusal: "My hour has not yet come" (verse 5). It was not yet time

206

for Him to begin His ministry and set in motion the events that would lead to the cross.

Despite this reply, Mary turned to the servants with great faith and wise advice: "Do whatever he tells you."

Just as with the Canaanite woman in Matthew 15:28, Jesus found Himself unable to resist such faith. In effect, Mary forced His hand! Her faith actually accelerated God's plan. Seeing six huge stone jars standing nearby, Jesus told the servants, "Fill the jars with water" (verse 7).

From a human point of view, however, this made no sense. The problem was not a lack of water, but a lack of wine. The servants could easily have grumbled or outright refused, thinking, *What a pointless command!* It was no easy job to fill these jars either, each holding twenty to thirty gallons. It probably meant numerous trips out to the village well, hauling up and lugging back heavy buckets, again and again. Yet these servants, on the strength of Mary's word, did what Jesus said and filled the jars to the brim. Their response was a model of prompt and enthusiastic obedience.

But before the miracle, another act of obedience was required. Now Jesus asked them to draw out some of the water and bring it to the steward of the feast. Again, this made no sense. Bringing a ladleful of *water* to a steward who was probably upset at the lack of wine could lead to embarrassment at best, or even a sharp rebuke. The gospel does not tell us that the water had already become wine when they brought it. Rather, it seems to have become wine at some point between their drawing it out and the steward tasting it. This second act of obedient faith opened the way for Jesus to work His first miracle.

Often, Jesus tells people to do something that does not make sense in the natural realm. He told a man with a withered hand to do the one thing he could not do: "Stretch out your hand." And the hand was healed (Luke 6:10). He told a lame man to do the impossible: "Get up, take up your bed, and walk." And at once the man was healed (John 5:8–9). He told the apostles to distribute a few loaves and fish to a crowd of thousands. In the course of distributing these totally inadequate provisions, the loaves and fish somehow multiplied (see Matthew 14:19).

So it is with us. Often, the Holy Spirit gives us light impressions or promptings that we are tempted to ignore because they don't seem to make sense. If we want to grow in the gifts, we need to decide to be radically obedient and trust that the Lord will use us—and even at times use our mistakes.

7. Know Your Authority in Christ

The centurion who begged Jesus to heal his servant understood something that other people did not. He said to Jesus,

> Lord, I am not worthy to have you come under my roof, but only say the word, and my servant will be healed. For I too am a man under authority, with soldiers under me. And I say to one, "Go," and he goes, and to another, "Come," and he comes, and to my servant, "Do this," and he does it.
>
> Matthew 8:8–9

It is the only occasion in the gospels where Jesus was astonished at what someone said to Him. This faithful military officer understood that he himself had authority to command others because he himself was under the authority of the

Roman Empire, and he likewise understood that in a similar way Jesus had unlimited power over demons, diseases and death because He lived His whole life under the Father's authority. Jesus said, "I can do nothing on my own. . . . I seek not my own will but the will of him who sent me" (John 5:30).[3]

Christians are meant to walk with the kind of confident authority that comes from knowing who Jesus is and who we are in Him. We are heirs of the Kingdom. The Lord has given us a share in His own kingly rule. Each one of us has a part in His mission to dismantle the kingdom of darkness and make the Kingdom of God present wherever we are. This kind of knowledge cannot come by study or learning (as helpful as these are), but only by revelation from the Holy Spirit. The more we receive that revelation—the more we know Jesus' absolute lordship over the whole universe, His victory over sin and death won on the cross, His unconditional love for every human being—the more faith we have. That faith enables us to use the gifts with confident authority.

Some of the greatest miracles happening today are taking place in one of the poorest countries of the world, Mozambique, among people who live in remote villages. They are uneducated and dirt poor. They have nothing and think nothing of themselves. But they know who they are in Christ, and God uses their humility and faith even to raise the dead.

8. Learn from Others

There is another irreplaceable kind of knowledge: the kind that comes from experience. It is one thing to read about the gifts and quite another to see them in operation, especially with people who have a lot of experience in using them.

It can be a great help to watch experienced people exercise a gift, and then sit down and discuss with them how they received the gift, how they exercised it, what the relationship was between God's revelation of His will and the operation of faith to bring it about, and the nuances of ministering in the gifts. These nuances are hard to explain in written form; it is best to watch someone ministering powerfully in the gifts and then ask questions to gain understanding.

Randy: This is what I had the privilege of doing with Blaine Cook, John Wimber and Omar Cabrera.

Mary: And this is what I have had the privilege of doing with Randy Clark, Damian Stayne and others.

9. Use Testimonies to Stir Up Faith

There is nothing that arouses faith in others like hearing the personal testimonies of people who have had their lives transformed by a healing, a miracle or another spiritual gift. Sometimes people are healed simply by hearing a testimony, even before there is prayer.

Mary: Recently in Argentina, I was about to lead a healing service. To help awaken people's faith, I shared a testimony about a friend of mine who prayed over a young girl in a wheelchair.[4] That girl, who had cerebral palsy, experienced a significant physical healing and also came to faith in Christ. As I was telling the story, there was a commotion in the back of the room, and a young girl came walking haltingly up the center aisle. She, too, had cerebral palsy, and as she heard that testimony, faith had risen up in her and she took the bold step of getting up to walk in front of everyone. Although she was not fully healed at that moment, she was walking with much greater ease and freedom from pain than she had ever had before.

10. Remove Obstacles and Misunderstandings

It is possible to exercise a powerful charism and yet have its effect blocked in the person to whom it is directed. Many people have mindsets that make it difficult for them to receive a healing or any other manifest work of God. People need help in putting off these misguided ways of thinking and letting their minds be filled with the truth revealed in Scripture.

For instance, some people have a deep-rooted sense that they are not worthy, that they don't deserve to be healed. The fact is, they are not worthy. No one is! But Jesus did not come to minister to the worthy; He came precisely for those who are not worthy, who are spiritually destitute and have nothing to offer Him (see Matthew 9:12–13). He is the Savior who loves to save. He has made us worthy by shedding His blood for us on the cross.

Others, especially Catholics, have the idea that it is better not to ask God for a healing, but just to accept your sickness and offer it up. But this is a distortion of the Catholic theology of redemptive suffering. It is true that "for those who love God all things work together for good, for those who are called according to his purpose" (Romans 8:28), and that suffering offered up in love, in union with Christ, has immeasurable value. But it does not follow that we should not ask for healing. What would you think of a doctor who diagnosed a patient with a serious illness and then said, "Sorry, I'm not going to treat you because it's better that you simply accept this sickness. Offer it up"? He would quickly lose his medical license! As we do not hesitate to seek earthly medical help, how much more should we seek help from Jesus, the Divine Physician?

Still others have a "name it, claim it" theology that can amount to manipulating God. We have to correct this mentality, helping people understand that God's gifts are truly gifts, not entitlements that we can demand on our terms. The Holy Spirit brings the fruit of self-control, never God-control (see Galatians 5:23).

Randy: I wrote an entire book that is dedicated to identifying teachings and practices that either hinder faith or help create faith for healing. The first half of the book identifies those things that create obstacles to healing and faith. The second half of the book discusses those things that build up faith and increase the probability of healings and miracles. The book's title is *The Healing Breakthrough*, and it is one of the most important books I've written on healing.[5]

11. Give the Holy Spirit Room to Work

The Lord loves to show His power, especially to those who are the most broken. Since the world is full of broken people, letting the Holy Spirit work means leaving room for "messiness." When frail human beings come into direct contact with the manifest presence of God, it is not always neat and tidy. They may fall to the floor, rest in the Spirit or react in other dramatic ways. We need to ask the Lord for wisdom and prudence to pastor the work of the Spirit in a way that avoids causing harm and yet allows the Spirit full freedom.

The Holy Spirit respects our free will, and He is sometimes constrained from acting by human plans that are rigid and inflexible. As Cardinal Ratzinger (later Pope Benedict XVI) wrote, bishops and other church leaders "must not turn their own pastoral plans into the criterion of what the Holy Spirit is allowed to do."[6] In organizing church events, if we want the Lord to act in power, we have to be willing to let Him do as He wills. That does not mean we don't make plans, but it does mean we are willing to change our plans at the drop of a hat if the Lord "shows up." Nor does it mean abdicating the responsibility for discernment, but it does mean that when we discern a sovereign movement of God, we subordinate our plans to His.

Mary: A friend once told me about a large Catholic conference held at a stadium in Canada. As the people were all worshiping together, the glory cloud of God's presence—what Jews call the *Shekinah*—became visible. As it moved through the stadium, people were being powerfully touched by the Holy Spirit. Some were being healed, others were being delivered from demonic oppression, and others were weeping in contrition for their sin. But because there was confusion and not everyone understood what was happening, the leaders decided to stop it quickly by having the music ministry start a song that interrupted the atmosphere of worship. The glory cloud immediately left. Sadly, instead of helping people understand and receive what the Lord was doing, these leaders blocked what He was doing.

12. Take It Out

Jesus taught His disciples the primary setting for the supernatural gifts of the Spirit: These gifts are to *accompany the proclamation of the Gospel* (see Mark 16:15–18). It is in evangelizing, in reaching the lost with the Good News of Christ, that the gifts are released with the greatest power.

World-renowned evangelist Billy Graham had this to say about the power of the Holy Spirit:

> I think it is a waste of time for us Christians to look for power we do not intend to use: for might in prayer, unless we pray; for strength to testify, without witnessing; for power unto holiness, without attempting to live a holy life; for grace to suffer, unless we take up the cross; for power in service, unless we serve. Someone has said, "God gives dying grace only to the dying."[7]

Pope Francis gave a similar message to Catholics:

> Spirit-filled evangelizers means evangelizers fearlessly open to the working of the Holy Spirit. At Pentecost, the Spirit made the apostles go forth from themselves. . . ."
>
> I prefer a Church which is bruised, hurting and dirty because it has been out on the streets, rather than a Church which is unhealthy from being confined and from clinging to its own security. . . . If something should rightly disturb us and trouble our consciences, it is the fact that so many of our brothers and sisters are living without the strength, light and consolation born of friendship with Jesus Christ.[8]

A church or a ministry that stays enclosed within its own four walls, ministering only to its own people week after week, will die out, just as the water of the Dead Sea stagnates, having no outlet. If we become a closed circle, we are not being the ambassadors of the Kingdom that the Lord calls us to be. But if we turn outward, compelled by the love of Christ, the Lord will delight in making His Kingdom manifest through us with signs, wonders, miracles and distributed gifts of the Holy Spirit.

We would like to conclude this chapter on activating and growing in the spiritual gifts—and indeed, conclude this whole book—with a prayer for you:

Father, in Jesus' name we ask You to release the gifts of Your Holy Spirit in a greater measure into the life of the one reading this book. We ask that You fill this reader afresh with Your Holy Spirit, open his or her spiritual eyes to see and spiritual ears to hear the cries of those all around who need You and who need the revelation of Your mercy, grace and power. We ask for the gifts to be released through this reader in order to display Your glory. We ask that You and Your Son would receive glory through the Holy Spirit's gift. We pray for a greater understanding of Your ways: how gifts of revelation release the gift of faith, and how the gift of faith releases the gifts of healings and working of miracles. We pray for humility and confidence to operate in this reader's life. We bless him or her in Jesus' powerful name. More, Lord! More love! More power! More of You in our lives! In the authority of Jesus' name, Amen and Amen.

Notes

Introduction

1. You can see the video testimony of this healing and others I mention throughout this book in the playlist at www.globalawakening.com/spiritualgiftshandbook. To strengthen faith for healing, there are extra videos to watch of more amazing stories there was not time or room to include here.

2. For more on these commonalities, see the report of the International Catholic–Pentecostal Dialogue, "'Do Not Quench the Spirit': Charisms in the Life and Mission of the Church," http://www.vatican.va/roman_curia/pontifical _councils/chrstuni/pentecostals/rc_pc_chrstuni_doc_2011-2015_do-not-quench -the-spirit_en.html.

3. Francis, apostolic exhortation *Evangelii Gaudium* [The Joy of the Gospel], November 24, 2013, 246.

Chapter 1: What Are Spiritual Gifts?

1. Novatian, *De Trinitate*, 29.9–10; quoted by Pope John Paul II, encyclical letter *Veritatis Splendor* [The Splendour of Truth], August 6, 1993, sec. 108.

2. See Romans 12:6–8; 1 Corinthians 12:4–10, 28–30; Ephesians 4:11–12; 1 Peter 4:10–11. There are also passages that list gifts of the Spirit without using the term *gift* or *charism*: Matthew 7:22–23; Mark 16:17–18; Acts 2:17–18; 4:30; 1 Corinthians 13:1–3; 14:6, 26–33.

3. The term was very rare in ancient Greek, apart from the writings of Paul. It occurs only in variants in the Septuagint (Sirach 7:23; 38:30; once in Theodotion at Psalm 30:22), and twice in the first-century Jewish philosopher Philo.

4. In 1 Corinthians 14:12 (NRSV) Paul uses a slightly different term: "Since you are eager for spiritual gifts [literally, "spirits"], strive to excel in them for building up the church."

Notes

5. In this book we will use the terms *spiritual gift* and *charism* synonymously, keeping in mind the fact that for Paul, the spiritual gifts seem to be a subset of charisms that depend in a particular way on inspiration by the Holy Spirit.

6. Because of the grammatical form of Ephesians 4:11, some biblical scholars actually view it as a list of four offices, with the last two terms referring to a single office of "pastor-teacher."

7. Later in the same part of the letter, Paul also adds gifts of teaching, helping and administration (1 Corinthians 12:28); giving to the poor and martyrdom (1 Corinthians 13:3); revelation and knowledge (1 Corinthians 14:6); an (inspired) hymn, a word of instruction and a revelation (1 Corinthians 14:26).

8. Catholic priest and theologian Raniero Cantalamessa, who has served as Preacher to the Papal Household since 1980, rightly cautions against overemphasizing the distinction between sanctifying gifts (traditionally called *gratiae gratum facientes*, graces that make us pleasing to God) and spiritual gifts (traditionally called *gratiae gratis datae*, graces freely given), since the converse is also true: Sanctifying gifts are given freely, and a spiritual gift put to good use makes us pleasing to God. See Cantalamessa, *Come, Creator Spirit: Meditations on the Veni Creator* (Collegeville, Minn.: Liturgical Press, 2003), 174.

9. Piety is not mentioned in the Hebrew of Isaiah 11:1–3, but is in the Septuagint and the Vulgate, the ancient Greek and Latin translations of the Old Testament.

10. *Catechism of the Catholic Church*, par. 1831.

11. Saint Thomas Aquinas, *Summa Theologica* II-II, q. 171–178, especially q. 178 a. 1.

12. See Cantalamessa, *Come, Creator Spirit*, 181.

13. John Paul II, "The Holy Spirit's Role in the Incarnation," general audience address, May 27, 1998.

14. See, for instance, Saint John of the Cross, *The Ascent of Mount Carmel*, III.31.

15. Ralph Martin, "Charismatic and Contemplative: What Would John of the Cross Say?" https://www.renewalministries.net/files/freeliterature/Char_Cont..pdf.

16. Saint John of the Cross, *The Ascent of Mount Carmel*, III.30.2.

17. Ibid., 30.3.

18. These three persons' stories are told in Randy Clark, *There Is More* (Chosen, 2013), which deals not only with the testimonies of many people who received such impartations, but also with the biblical basis for a belief in such experiences today, in the twenty-first century.

19. This is still happening so much that I have written two other books that deal with the stories of fishermen, Catholic priests, Episcopal priests, Protestant pastors, housewives, vice presidents of banks, doctors, people like you and me—just "little ole me's." Those two books are *Changed in a Moment* (Global Awakening, 2010) and *God Can Use Little Ole Me* (Destiny Image, 1998; out of print).

Chapter 2: The Spirit of the Lord Is upon Me

1. Throughout the gospel of Luke, going in haste is a sign of joy at the presence of Jesus. The shepherds come to Bethlehem "in haste" to see the newborn king; Zacchaeus comes down from the tree "in haste" to meet Jesus.

218

2. From *A Word in Season: Readings for the Liturgy of the Hours*, VII (Villanova, Pa.: Augustinian Press, 1999), 245.

3. See Matthew 12:38; 16:1, 22–23.

4. Theophilus, *Ad Autolycum* 1.12 (*Patrologia Graeca* 6.1041). The Greek word for "Christian" comes from the verb *anoint*.

5. Saint Thomas Aquinas, *Summa Theologica* III, q. 7, a. 7.

6. See also Luke 7:16; 9:8, 19; 24:19.

7. See Acts 2:41; 4:4; 5:12; 21:20; Romans 15:19.

Chapter 3: Clothed with Power

1. See Matthew 28:16–20; Mark 16:15–18; Luke 24:46–49.

2. R. P. Menzies, *The Development of Early Christian Pneumatology with Special Reverence to Luke–Acts*, JSNT Supplement Series 54 (Sheffield University Press, 1991), as quoted in Jon Ruthven, *On the Cessation of the Charismata: A Protestant Polemic on Post-biblical Miracles* (Tulsa, Okla.: Word & Spirit Press, 2011), 99–100n8.

3. See Matthew 14:34–36; Mark 5:27; 7:25.

4. Rodney Stark, *The Rise of Christianity: How the Obscure, Marginal Jesus Movement Became the Dominant Religious Force in the Western World in a Few Centuries* (San Francisco: HarperSanFrancisco, 1996), 4–13.

5. Ibid., 73–128, 147–62.

6. Ramsay MacMullen, *Christianizing the Roman Empire A.D. 100–400* (New Haven, Conn.: Yale University Press, 1984), 27–28.

7. Irenaeus, *Against Heresies*, 2.32.4.

8. Saint Justin Martyr, *Second Apology*, 6.5–6.

9. Origen, *Against Celsus*, 7.4.

10. See Kilian McDonnell, "Evangelization and the Experience of Initiation in the Early Church," in *John Paul II and the New Evangelization: How You Can Bring the Good News to Others*, rev. ed. (Cincinnati: Servant, 2006), 79–93. This article summarizes the more detailed study by Kilian McDonnell and George T. Montague, *Christian Initiation and Baptism in the Holy Spirit: Evidence from the First Eight Centuries*, rev. ed. (Collegeville, Minn.: Liturgical Press, 1994).

11. Cyprian, *Treatise to Donatus on the Grace of God*, paraphrased by Anne Field in *From Darkness to Light: What It Meant to Become a Christian in the Early Church* (Ann Arbor, Mich.: Servant, 1978), 190–92.

12. Tertullian, *On Baptism,* 20.

13. McDonnell, "Evangelization," 84.

14. Cyril, *Catechetical Lectures*, 16.12.

15. Cyril, *Catechetical Lectures*, 17.19; 17.37; 18.32.

16. Hilary, *Tract on the Psalms*, 64.14–15.

17. Augustine, *City of God*, XXII.8.

18. Ibid.

19. Irenaeus, *Against Heresies*, 5.6.1.

20. Ibid., 3.11.9.

21. Justin Martyr, *Dialogue with Trypho*, 82.

22. Cyprian, *Letter 16* [9].4.1.

23. Cyprian, *Letter* 39 [33].1.1–2. Likewise Numidicus, a man whose wife had been martyred, was chosen for the clergy by prophetic revelation (*Letter* 40 [34].1.1).

24. Tertullian, *A Treatise on the Soul*, 9:3–4.

25. *The Passion of the Holy Martyrs Perpetua and Felicity*, 3.

26. Socrates of Constantinople, *Church History*, IV.27; see also Basil, *On the Holy Spirit*, 74.

27. Basil, *On the Holy Spirit*, 74.

28. Augustine, *On the Psalms*, 99.3.

29. Ibid., 97.4.

30. Gregory the Great, *Moralia in Job*, 24.10; cf. 28.35.

31. Chrysostom, *Homily on the Great Week*.

32. John Cassian, *First Conference of Abbot Isaac, On Prayer*, 14, 27.

33. A few of the more famous healers of the twentieth century would be Alexander Dowy, John G. Lake, Aimee Simple-McPherson, Kathryn Kuhlman, Charles Price, A. A. Allen, Jack Coe, William Branham, T. L. Osborn, Oral Roberts and Benson Idahosa. Some of the healers of the twenty-first century would be Enoch Adeboye, Reinhard Bonnke, Benny Hinn, Henry Madava, Leif Hetland, Heidi Baker and Bill Johnson. (There are many more famous healers in Africa and Asia, but space and time do not permit a listing.)

34. As quoted in Raniero Cantalamessa, *Sober Intoxication of the Spirit*, trans. Marsha Daigle-Williamson (Cincinnati: Servant, 2005), 1.

35. Cyril of Jerusalem, from *Catechetical Lectures*, 17.19, as quoted in Cantalamessa, *Sober Intoxication*, 2–3.

36. Augustine, *Sermon* 225.4; emphasis added.

37. Augustine, *Sermon* 24.1 (translation adapted from Augustine, *Sermons [20–50]: On the Old Testament*, trans. Edmund Hill, OP, ed. John E. Rotelle, Works of Saint Augustine III/2 [Brooklyn, New York: New City Press, 1990], 72).

38. Saint Thomas Aquinas, *In Psalterium*, Ps 35[36]:9.

39. John Ruusbroec, *The Spiritual Espousals and Other Works*, trans. James A. Wiseman, OSB, The Classics of Western Spirituality (Mahwah, N.J.: Paulist Press, 1985), 82–83.

40. Salimbene di Adam, in *Monumenta Germaniae*, vol. XXXII, Scriptores, 70, quoted in Eddie Ensley, *Sounds of Wonder: 20 Centuries of Praying in Tongues and Lively Worship in the Catholic Tradition* (Phoenix: Tau Publishing, 2013), 77.

41. See Mary Crawford, *The Shantung Revival* (Mechanicsburg, Pa.: Global Awakening, 2005).

Chapter 4: Fire on the Earth

1. See Acts 2:38; 8:14–16; 9:17; 10:44; 11:15–16; 19:6.

2. Pope Leo XIII, encyclical letter *Divinum Illud Munus*, May 9, 1897.

3. It is known to be nine days because Jesus ascended into heaven forty days after His resurrection (see Acts 1:3), and the Holy Spirit descended on the Jewish feast of Pentecost, which is fifty days after Passover Sabbath (when Jesus was in the tomb).

4. John Paul II, "Message of Pope John Paul II for the World Congress of the Ecclesial Movements and New Communities," May 27, 1998.

5. Vatican Council II, Dogmatic Constitution on the Church (*Lumen Gentium*), November 21, 1964, 12.

6. The story of this retreat, including personal testimonies from many of the participants, is told in Patti Gallagher Mansfield, *As by a New Pentecost: The Dramatic Beginning of the Catholic Charismatic Renewal* (Phoenix: Amor Deus Publishing, 2016).

7. Mansfield, *As by a New Pentecost*, 55.

8. In 2001, David Barrett, George Thomas Kurian and Todd M. Johnson estimated the number at 120 million. See *World Christian Encyclopedia: A Comparative Survey of Churches and Religions in the Modern World*, 2nd ed. (Oxford: Oxford University Press, 2001).

9. For more on Catholic views of baptism in the Spirit, see Doctrinal Commission of International Catholic Charismatic Renewal Services, *Baptism in the Holy Spirit* (Vatican City: ICCRS, 2012); Mary Healy, co-author.

10. In 2007, this organization became known as the Holy Spirit Renewal Ministries, broadening itself to include non-American Baptists.

11. Dr. Robert Culpepper, a Southern Baptist professor of theology in Japan, also held this view. He wrote of the need to appropriate by faith all that we have already through our new birth. See Culpepper, *An Evaluation of the Charismatic Movement: A Theological and Biblical Appraisal* (Valley Forge, Pa.: Judson Press, 1977).

12. Gordon D. Fee, *Gospel and Spirit: Issues in New Testament Hermeneutics* (Peabody, Mass.: Hendrickson, 1991), 105–19.

13. See Léon Joseph Suenens, *A New Pentecost?* (San Francisco: Harper, 1984); Raniero Cantalamessa, *Sober Intoxication of the Spirit: Filled with the Fullness of God*, trans. Marsha Daigle-Williamson (Cincinnati: Servant, 2005), 38–57; Ralph Martin, "Catholic Theology and 'Baptism in the Spirit,'" *Logos: A Journal of Catholic Thought and Culture* 14:3 (2011), 17–43.

14. According to Catholic teaching, grace is objectively given through the sacraments, but the sacraments do not produce their intended results automatically. Faith is needed in order for the power of God to operate through the sacrament to actually transform a person's life. See the *Catechism of the Catholic Church*, pars. 1128 and 2111.

15. See Raniero Cantalamessa, "The Baptism in the Spirit, A Grace for the Whole Church," Norfolk, Va., May 2014, https://zenit.org/articles/father-cant alamessa-explains-why-baptism-in-the-spirit-is-a-gift-for-the-whole-church/.

16. This separation occurred in the western (Latin Rite) Catholic Church, though not in the Orthodox or the Eastern Catholic Churches, which continued to administer the sacrament of confirmation immediately after baptism, through an anointing with sacred oil (chrism).

17. See Stephen B. Clark, *Confirmation and the "Baptism of the Holy Spirit"* (Pecos, N.Mex.: Dove, 1969).

18. *Catechism of the Catholic Church*, par. 1302.

19. Francis Sullivan, SJ, *Charisms and Charismatic Renewal: A Biblical and Theological Study* (Eugene, Ore.: Wipf and Stock, 1982), 59–75. The German Catholic theologian Norbert Baumert takes a similar view.

20. Saint Thomas Aquinas, *Summa Theologica* I, q. 43, a. 6 ad 2.

21. You can hear Marcelo tell the story of his anointing at https://www.youtube.com/watch?v=-KQYX3UIZak.

22. In three of my books, I talk about people who received in this way, where a baptism in the Spirit also involved an impartation or activation of a gift. (See *There Is More, Changed in a Moment,* and *God Can Use Little Ole Me.*) This catapulted them into a new ministry or mission, or a much greater anointing in their ministry, with much more fruit.

23. Peter Hocken, "Baptized in the Spirit: An Eschatological Concept," *Journal of Pentecostal Theology* 13.2 (2005), 257–68.

24. See Acts 2:1–11; 4:31; 8:14–19; 9:17–18; 10:44–46; 19:6.

25. Charles H. Spurgeon, "The Power of the Holy Spirit," vol. 1 of *Spurgeon's Sermons* (Grand Rapids, Mich.: Baker, 1996), 129–30.

26. Paul VI, in his address to the 3rd International Congress of the Catholic Charismatic Renewal, May 19, 1975.

27. See Kilian McDonnell, ed., *Presence, Power, Praise: Documents on the Charismatic Renewal,* 3 vols. (Collegeville, Minn.: Liturgical Press, 1980).

28. John Paul II, address to a delegation of the renewal in the Holy Spirit movement, March 14, 2002; Benedict XVI, general audience, Sept. 28, 2005.

29. Francis, address to participants in the 37th National Convocation of the Renewal in the Holy Spirit, June 1, 2014.

30. R. A. Torrey, *The Baptism with the Holy Spirit* (Minneapolis: Bethany Fellowship, 1972), 39.

31. Ibid., 44.

32. Ibid., 52.

33. A. W. Tozer, *How to Be Filled with the Holy Spirit* (Camp Hill, Pa.: Christian Publications, n.d.), 39.

34. Neither Torrey nor Tozer explicitly discusses speaking this language. Scripture does not indicate that one must necessarily speak in tongues to have been baptized with the Spirit, although it is a common sign of an infilling.

35. Don Basham, *A Handbook on Holy Spirit Baptism* (Monroeville, Pa.: Whitaker Books, 1969), 100–109.

36. Doctrinal Commission of International Catholic Charismatic Renewal Services, *Baptism in the Holy Spirit: Jubilee Edition* (Rome: ICCRS, 2017).

37. See my book *There Is More* for details of this powerful experience and the manifestations that accompanied it.

Chapter 5: Revelation Gifts

1. As mentioned earlier, prophecy, tongues and interpretation also depend on revelation from God, but they more directly involve speech.

2. To learn about the seven ways someone can receive a word of knowledge, see Randy Clark, *Ministry Team Training Manual* (Global Awakening, 2012), or the little booklet *Words of Knowledge* (Global Awakening, 2011), also by Randy Clark.

3. You can see the video testimony of this woman's healing in the playlist at www.globalawakening.com/spiritualgiftshandbook.

Chapter 6: Power Gifts

1. For more on this subject see Randy Clark, *Authority to Heal: Restoring the Lost Inheritance of God's Healing Power* (Destiny Image, 2016).

2. For more on the gift of healing from a Catholic perspective, see Mary Healy, *Healing: Bringing the Gift of God's Mercy to the World* (Huntington, Ind.: OSV, 2015).

3. You can see the video testimony of this healing, and also follow-up testimony from four years later that talks about the impact the healing had on the man's family, in the first video in the playlist at www.globalawakening.com/spiritualgiftshandbook.

4. You can see the video testimony of this girl walking after her braces are taken off in the playlist at www.globalawakening.com/spiritualgiftshandbook. I tell many more such stories in my book *Eyewitness to Miracles* (Thomas Nelson, 2018). If I continued writing about miracles and healings here, this book would become far too long!

Chapter 7: Gifts of Speech

1. See Romans 12:6–8; 1 Corinthians 12:8–10, 28–30; 13:1–3; Ephesians 4:11; see also 1 Peter 4:10–11.

2. See Acts 9:10–12; 10:1–3, 17, 19; 12:9; 16:9–10; 18:9.

3. It is unusual for prophetic words to be given at Mass, although it does occur in some Masses in the Catholic Charismatic Renewal. These prophecies are usually submitted to discernment beforehand, and are given either during the homily or during a time of prayer after Holy Communion, always with full respect for Catholic liturgical norms.

4. Saint Bernard of Clairvaux, *On the Song of Songs*, III, sermon 56.7.

5. Simon Tugwell, ed., *Albert and Thomas: Selected Writings*, Classics of Western Spirituality (New York: Paulist Press, 1988), 380.

6. Saint Thomas Aquinas, *In Psalterium*, Ps 32.3.

7. Saint Teresa of Avila, *Interior Castle*, VI.6.10–11.

8. Abbé Francis Trochu, *The Curé d'Ars*, trans. Ernest Graf (Rockford, Ill.: Tan Books, 1977), 529–30.

9. See also Matthew 24:11; 2 Peter 2:1; 1 John 4:1; Revelation 16:13.

10. See https://www.renewalministries.net/files/freeliterature/Prophecy_KansasCity_1977.pdf.

11. John Chrysostom, *Six Books on the Priesthood*, trans. G. W. Butterworth (Crestwood, New York: St. Vladimir's Seminary Press, 1964), 44.

Chapter 8: Activating the Spiritual Gifts

1. For more on this subject, see Randy Clark, *There Is More: The Secret to Experiencing God's Power to Change Your Life* (Chosen, 2013). See also *Changed in a Moment* (Global Awakening, 2010), as well as *God Can Use Little Ole Me:*

Remarkable Stories of Ordinary Christians (Destiny Image, 1998; out of print), which also contains many testimonies of people whose lives were transformed and activated in gifts through an impartation.

2. See Matthew 9:36; 14:14; 15:32; 18:27; 20:34; Mark 1:41; 6:34; 8:2; Luke 7:13; 10:33; 15:20.

3. Cf. John 6:38; 8:28; 12:49; 14:10.

4. This story is told in Mary Healy, *Healing: Bringing the Gift of God's Mercy to the World* (Our Sunday Visitor, 2015).

5. See Randy Clark, *The Healing Breakthrough: Creating an Atmosphere of Faith for Healing* (Chosen, 2016), as well as *Authority to Heal: Restoring the Lost Inheritance of God's Healing Power* (Destiny Image, 2016), also by Randy Clark, and our Global Certification Program (GCP) at classroom.globalawakening.com.

6. Joseph Ratzinger, "The Ecclesial Movements: A Theological Reflection on Their Place in the Church," in *Movements in the Church: Proceedings of the World Congress of the Ecclesial Movements* (Vatican City: *Pontificium Consilium pro Laicis*, 1999), 23–51.

7. Billy Graham, *The Holy Spirit: Activating God's Power in Your Life* (Nashville: Thomas Nelson, 2000), 107.

8. Francis, apostolic exhortation *Evangelii Gaudium* [The Joy of the Gospel], November 24, 2013, sec. 259.

Index

Randy Clark is best known for helping to spark the move of God now affectionately labeled "the Toronto Blessing." In the years since, his influence has grown as an international speaker. He continues, with great tenacity, to demonstrate the Lord's power to heal the sick.

Randy received his M.Div. from The Southern Baptist Theological Seminary and his D.Min. from United Theological Seminary (Dayton, Ohio). He has written over forty books, and his message is simple: "God wants to use you."

The most important aspect of his calling to ministry is the way God uses him for impartation. John Wimber heard God speak audibly the first two times he met Randy, telling John that Randy would one day go around the world laying his hands on pastors and leaders for the impartation and activation of the gifts of the Holy Spirit. In January 1994, in the early days of the outpouring of the Spirit in Toronto, John called Randy and told him that what God had shown him about Randy a decade earlier was beginning now. It has continued ever since.

Randy has the unique ability to minister to many denominations and apostolic networks. These have included Roman Catholics, Messianic Jews, Methodists, Reformed Lutheran, many Pentecostal and charismatic congregations, and the largest Baptist churches in Argentina, Brazil and South Africa.

He has also taken several thousand people with him on international ministry teams. Bill Johnson says the fastest way to increase in the supernatural is to accompany Randy on an international trip. Randy has traveled to over 54 countries and continues to travel extensively to see that God's mandate on his life is fulfilled.

Randy and his wife, DeAnne, reside in Mechanicsburg, Pennsylvania. They have four adult children, all married, and six grandchildren. For more information about Randy Clark, his ministry and his resource materials, visit www.globalawakening.com. To invite Dr. Randy Clark to minister, contact his personal assistant, vicki@globalawakening.com.

Dr. Mary Healy is professor of Scripture at Sacred Heart Major Seminary in Detroit, Michigan. She gives talks and leads healing services at conferences around the world. Her mission is twofold: to help Catholics and all Christians fall in love with the Word of God, and to open people's hearts to the full power and gifts of the Holy Spirit.

Mary received her doctorate in biblical theology from the Pontifical Gregorian University in Rome. She is a general editor of the Catholic Commentary on Sacred Scripture, a series of commentaries that interpret Scripture from the heart of the Church, and author of two of its volumes. She serves as chair of the Doctrinal Commission of International Catholic Charismatic Renewal Services in Rome. She also serves the Pontifical Council for Promoting Christian Unity as a member of the Pentecostal-Catholic International Dialogue. Mary was appointed by Pope Francis as one of the first three women ever to serve on the Pontifical Biblical Commission.

More dynamic teaching from Randy Clark!

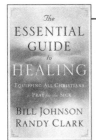
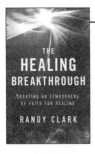